23-

D1269480

Historical Atlases of South Asia,
Central Asia, and the Middle East™

A HISTORICAL ATLAS OF

EGYPT

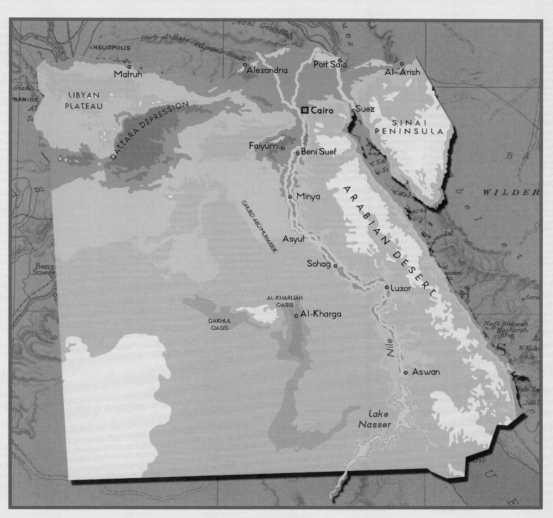

Allison Stark Draper

The Rosen Publishing Group, Inc., New York

Published in 2004 by The Rosen Publishing Group, Inc.
29 East 21st Street, New York, NY 10010

Copyright © 2004 by The Rosen Publishing Group, Inc.

First Edition

Library of Congress Cataloging-in-Publication Data

Draper, Allison Stark.
A historical atlas of Egypt / Allison Stark Draper.—1st ed.
p. cm. — (Historical Atlases of South Asia, Central Asia, and the Middle East)
Summary: Maps and text chronicle the history of Egypt, which became a civilized land some 5000 years ago.
Includes bibliographical references and index.
Contents: The geography of Egypt — Ancient Egypt — Greece, Rome, and Byzantium — The Arab invasion — The Mamluks and the Ottomans — Napoleon and Egyptology — Egypt becomes a nation — The Arab Republic of Egypt.
ISBN 0-8239-4498-0 (lib. bdg.)
1. Egypt—History—Maps for children. 2. Egypt—Maps for children. [1. Egypt—History.
2. Atlases.] I. Title. II. Series.
G2491.S1D7 2004
911'.62—dc22

2003055018

Manufactured in the United States of America

Cover images: Current Egyptian president Hosni Mubarak *(top left)*, a relief sculpture of an ancient Egyptian prisoner *(right)*, and a nineteenth-century painting of Muhammad Ali, pasha of Egypt from 1806 until 1848 *(bottom left)*, each rest atop a contemporary map of Egypt and a historic eighteenth-century map of Egypt and the Sinai Peninsula.

Contents

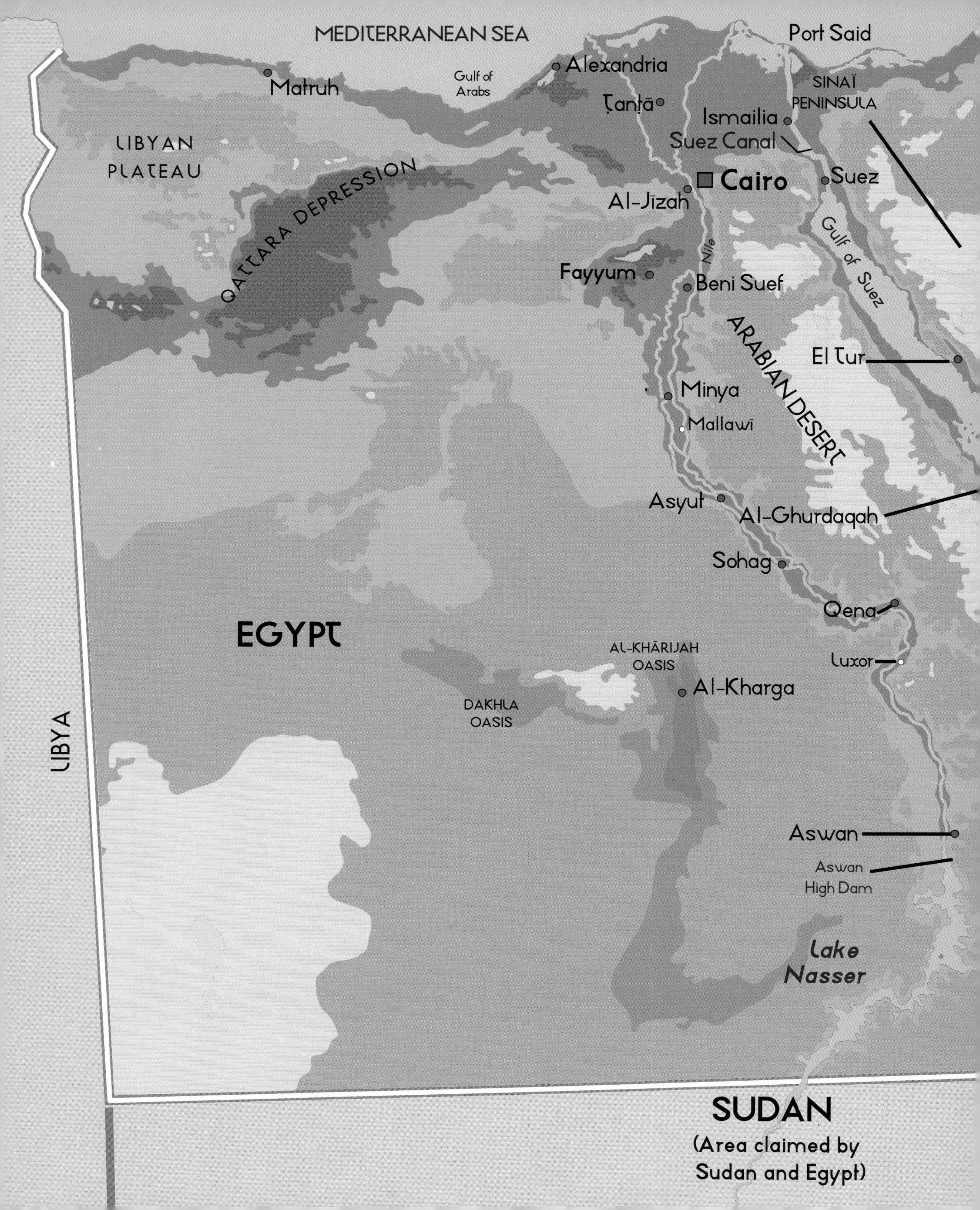

MEDITERRANEAN SEA

Port Said

• Alexandria

Gulf of
Arabs

Maṭruh

Ṭanṭā

SINAÏ
PENINSULA

Ismailia

Suez Canal

LIBYAN
PLATEAU

QATTARA DEPRESSION

□ **Cairo**

Suez

Al-Jīzah

Nile

Gulf of Suez

Fayyum

Beni Suef

ARABIAN DESERT

El Tur

Minya

Mallawī

Asyut

Al-Ghurdaqah

Sohag

EGYPT

Qena

AL-KHĀRIJAH
OASIS

Luxor

Al-Kharga

DAKHLA
OASIS

LIBYA

Aswan

Aswan
High Dam

*Lake
Nasser*

SUDAN
(Area claimed by
Sudan and Egypt)

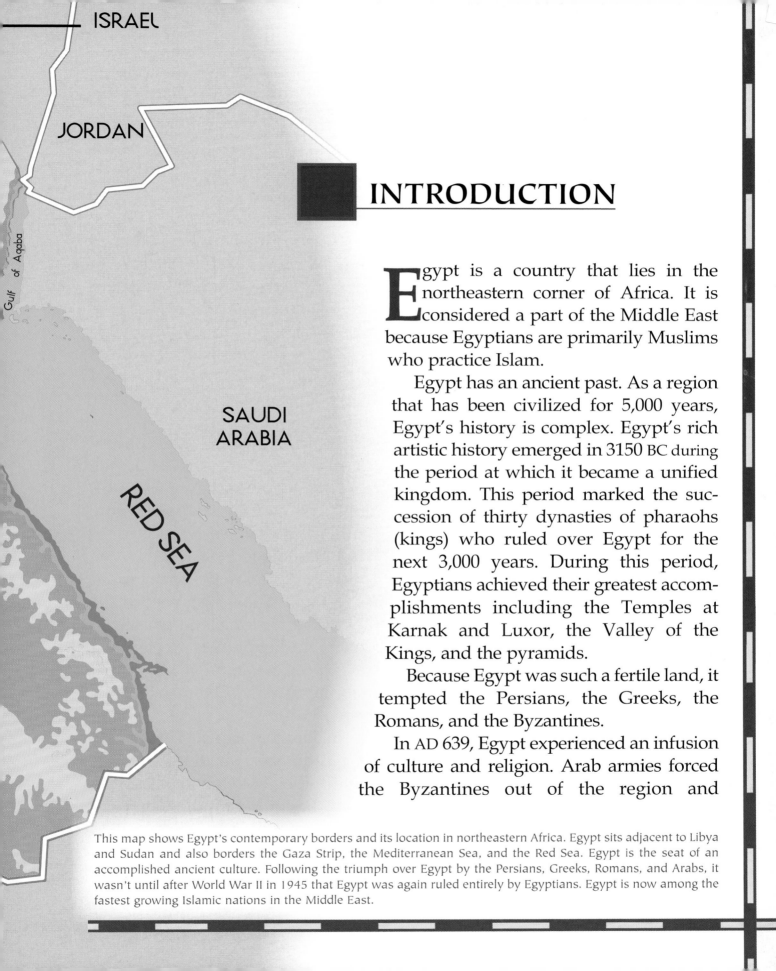

ISRAEL

JORDAN

Gulf of Aqaba

SAUDI
ARABIA

RED SEA

INTRODUCTION

Egypt is a country that lies in the northeastern corner of Africa. It is considered a part of the Middle East because Egyptians are primarily Muslims who practice Islam.

Egypt has an ancient past. As a region that has been civilized for 5,000 years, Egypt's history is complex. Egypt's rich artistic history emerged in 3150 BC during the period at which it became a unified kingdom. This period marked the succession of thirty dynasties of pharaohs (kings) who ruled over Egypt for the next 3,000 years. During this period, Egyptians achieved their greatest accomplishments including the Temples at Karnak and Luxor, the Valley of the Kings, and the pyramids.

Because Egypt was such a fertile land, it tempted the Persians, the Greeks, the Romans, and the Byzantines.

In AD 639, Egypt experienced an infusion of culture and religion. Arab armies forced the Byzantines out of the region and

This map shows Egypt's contemporary borders and its location in northeastern Africa. Egypt sits adjacent to Libya and Sudan and also borders the Gaza Strip, the Mediterranean Sea, and the Red Sea. Egypt is the seat of an accomplished ancient culture. Following the triumph over Egypt by the Persians, Greeks, Romans, and Arabs, it wasn't until after World War II in 1945 that Egypt was again ruled entirely by Egyptians. Egypt is now among the fastest growing Islamic nations in the Middle East.

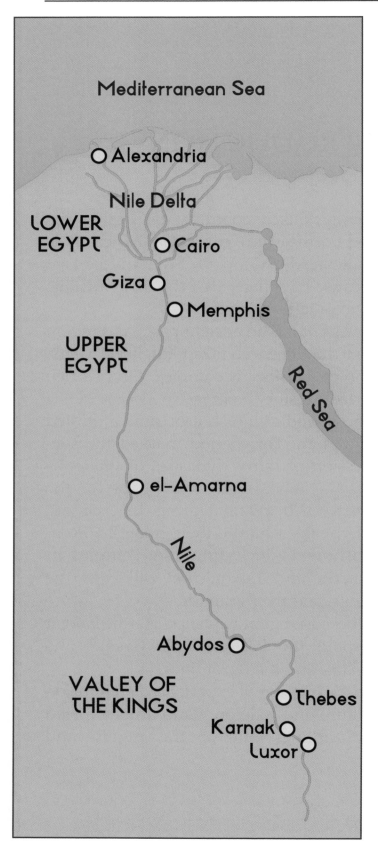

Mediterranean Sea

O Alexandria

Nile Delta

LOWER
EGYPT

O Cairo

Giza O

O Memphis

UPPER
EGYPT

Red Sea

O el-Amarna

Nile

Abydos O

VALLEY OF
THE KINGS

O Thebes

Karnak O

Luxor O

This map of ancient Egypt shows the Nile River and the division between Lower and Upper Egypt. There were many differences between these two regions during ancient times, including variations in dialect, customs, and daily activities. Today, Lower Egypt, or northern Egypt, extends from present-day Cairo to the Nile delta in Alexandria. Contemporary Upper Egypt, or southern Egypt, extends from present-day Aswan to just south of Cairo.

introduced Christian Egyptians to Islam. Although Arab dominance in Egypt marked a period of independence, Mamluks (slave warriors) conquered Egypt in 1250. This occupation was followed by a defeat by Ottoman Turks in 1517. Egypt then became part of the Islamic Ottoman Empire.

Napoléon invaded the country and captured Cairo in 1798. In the years that followed, Egypt became a center of world transportation, allowing traders easier access to prized Asian goods.

British control in Egypt increased in the 1880s. The British needed the Suez Canal for trade and wanted to protect it. Egypt was declared a British protectorate in 1914. At that time, the Turkish Ottoman Empire entered World War I on the German side, making Britain and Turkey enemies. After the war, the Egyptians wanted their independence from Britain. Egypt became independent in 1922, but British officers occupied the country until 1936. Egypt then became known as the Arab Republic of Egypt in 1952, as it is known today.

1 THE GEOGRAPHY OF EGYPT

It is difficult to understand the history of Egypt without a complete understanding of its Nile River and the fertile Nile Valley. The Nile River was, in fact, the main reason for Egypt becoming a prosperous kingdom early in recorded human history.

The Nile River, some 4,000 miles (6,700 kilometers) long, was the only waterway to flow across the Sahara Desert. In fact, it was the vital artery that linked Upper and Lower Egypt. Historically, Upper Egypt extended from Aswan in the south to present-day Cairo. Lower Egypt spread from the point where the Nile fanned into a triangular delta before reaching the Mediterranean Sea. The Nile's yearly summer flood carried rich black sediment north, allowing the ancient Egyptians to farm successfully with little rainfall. A series of irrigation canals carried excess water to nearby farmlands. Egyptians called their kingdom Kemet, or the "Black Land," because of the fertile black silt left on the soil after these floods.

With careful irrigation, the Egyptians could produce two harvests a year in some areas. This was more food than the kingdom needed. This surplus allowed Egyptians to trade for luxuries from other lands. It also supported a sophisticated culture of scholars, architects, priests, and doctors.

Kemet

The name "Egypt" dates from the invasion of the Macedonian conqueror Alexander the Great (ruled 332–323 BC). The ancient Nile Valley name for the temple of Ptah at Memphis, a city in Lower Egypt, was Haikuptah, or the "House of the Soul of Ptah." Alexander's soldiers mispronounced it "Aigyptos," which eventually became "Egypt." The people of the land called it Kemet, because of its rich black-colored soil. Throughout the rest of the Semitic-speaking Middle East, Egypt was called Misr, the name it still bears in Arabic.

This historical map of the Nile River is based on observations made by the fifth century BC Greek historian Herodotus, who traveled widely in Egypt during his lifetime.

Ancient Egypt was a narrow territory in North Africa that widened into the delta where the Nile meets the sea. In both Lower and Upper Egypt, desert lay to the east and west of the Nile River. In the south, there were cataracts, or descending waterfalls or rapids, where boats could not navigate. These geographical boundaries protected the Egyptians and isolated them from the rest of Africa.

Today, modern Egypt is a rough square with 1,470 miles (2,365 km) of coastline in the southeastern corner of the Mediterranean. Its straight western and southern boundaries border Libya and Sudan while its eastern side runs northwest along the Red Sea. Its northeast corner, across what is now the Suez Canal, borders Israel and the Gaza Strip.

The Nile

The upper part of the Nile, where it emerges from Africa, is called the White Nile. At Khartoum, Sudan, it joins the Blue Nile, which rushes down from the highlands of Abyssinia (Ethiopia). About 140 miles (225 km) north of this point, the Nile meets the Atbara, the only other stream to join it. Just below Khartoum, the Nile enters the land of sandstone under the Sahara Desert. Stone cataracts churn the glassy Nile into froth at six points. These six cataracts lie between Khartoum and Aswan. Each consists of large rocky masses the water cannot erode. No one cataract is high enough to create a major waterfall. The first, second, and fourth cataracts are too dangerous to navigate. The first (and northernmost) is a granite barrier at Elephantine. North of this, the river runs smoothly to the Mediterranean Sea.

In ancient times, the valley north of the first cataract was Egypt proper. At Edfu, 68 miles (109 km) north of this cataract, the sandstone changes to softer limestone. This change allowed the river to erode a vast canyon that extends north toward the sea. The high cliffs it created run north-south on either side and extend to about 10 miles (17 km) across. Flowing north, the river moves 3 miles (5 km) an hour and twice reaches its greatest width of 1,100 yards (1,045 meters).

The river's banks are low and flat. In earlier times, Nile floods filled most of the canyon between the cliffs. In the few places the cliffs stood beyond the reach of the floodwaters, low desert or red land bordered the fertile black land. The line between the two was abrupt. During ancient times it was possible to stand with one foot on the lush greenery of the valley and the other on the desert sand.

Centuries later in 1902, British-occupied Egypt dammed the Nile at Aswan to control the water supply for farming. By the 1970s, Egyptians used similar technology to rebuild the dam, creating Aswan High Dam and Lake Nasser, which is the second-largest

Climate

The air of Egypt, like that of the surrounding deserts, is warm, dry, and clear. Upper Egypt receives about 1 inch (2.5 centimeters) of rain every ten years. Rare showers sometimes occur in gigantic cloudbursts and always come out of the west. The ancient Egyptians regarded rainfall as a curse and an inferior method of irrigation sent by the gods to less favored lands. The Delta receives 8 inches (20 cm) of rain annually, but desert winds blow from the south and dry the air. This protects the marshy Delta from malaria, which is common in other parts of tropical Africa.

The German cartographer Sebastian Munster designed this woodcut of Egypt's Nile River delta for his manuscript *Cosmographia*, which first appeared in 1544. The map designated the ancient cities Alexandria, Cairum, and Memphis, as well as the pyramids, which were represented by three square obelisks. This map is now located in the Library of the Decorative Arts in Paris, France.

artificial reservoir in the world. This provides a constant controllable water supply even during times of drought but prevents the annual flooding that once enriched the valley soil during ancient times.

The cliffs along the Nile range from a few hundred to a thousand feet high. To the west in Libya, the rock and gravel of the great Sahara border the fertile Egyptian valley. The only water in this region is a scattered line of oases that follows the path of the Nile. During ancient times, the rock wall between the valley and the largest of these oases disintegrated. This created the fertile area of the Fayyum. To the east lies the Arabian Desert.

Eighty miles (129 km) from the Mediterranean, the Nile enters the north-facing triangle of the Delta. The point of the Delta lies just north of the ancient city of Memphis. In prehistoric times, this was a wide bay. Over time, the river filled it with silt. The Nile of the ancient Egyptians reached the sea through several streams. Today it splits into two main branches. The western is the Rosetta and the eastern is the Damiette. Until the massive dams of the twentieth century were built, floods gradually raised the level of the land. The river's path has changed, too; today, it winds through the valley more than a mile (1.6 km) east of the course it followed 2,000 years ago.

2 ANCIENT EGYPT

Early human settlements in Egypt grew into Upper and Lower Egypt. Upper Egypt was likely ruled by a king at Hierakonpolis and Lower Egypt by a king at Buto (modern-day Tell el-Fara'in). Around 3150 BC, King Narmer of Upper Egypt united the two regions. His successor, King Aha, then established the capital of unified Egypt in Memphis.

It was about this time that writing first appeared in Egypt. It seems to have been an Egyptian invention because its symbols, or hieroglyphics, are entirely Egyptian. The Egyptians became masters of this new art, keeping careful records of reigning pharaohs and the transfer of land. The beginning of Egypt's written history coincides almost exactly with the start of dynastic Egypt. Egypt's thirty dynasties are commonly grouped into three major periods: the Old Kingdom (2686–2160 BC), the Middle Kingdom (2040–1750 BC), and the New Kingdom (1550–1086 BC).

The Old Kingdom

The prosperous first dynasty of the Old Kingdom lasted 200 years. Each ruler had a tomb at Abydos in Lower Egypt and at Saqqara near Memphis, in the Valley of the Kings. It is impossible to say which contained the corpses as none have been excavated intact.

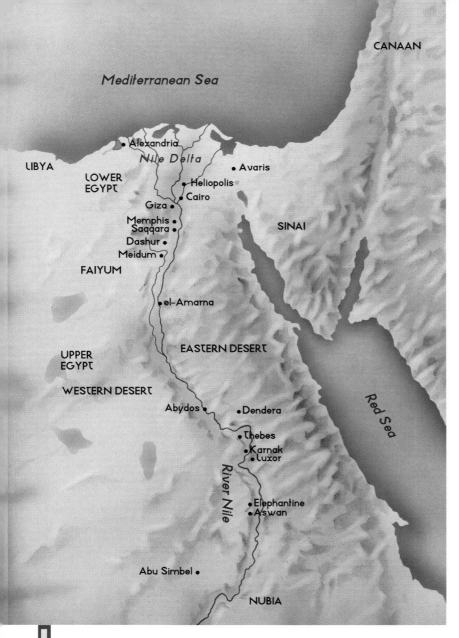

Map labels:
CANAAN
Mediterranean Sea
LIBYA
Alexandria
Nile Delta
LOWER EGYPT
Avaris
Heliopolis
Cairo
Giza
Memphis
Saqqara
Dashur
Meidum
SINAI
FAIYUM
el-Amarna
EASTERN DESERT
UPPER EGYPT
WESTERN DESERT
Abydos
Dendera
Thebes
Karnak
Luxor
Red Sea
River Nile
Elephantine
Aswan
Abu Simbel
NUBIA

Ancient Egypt is depicted in this map designed by a contemporary artist in 2003. The city of Memphis, seen here in Lower Egypt at the tip of the Nile delta, was the capital of the Old Kingdom (3100-2258 BC). Menes (Narmer), the first king of united Egypt, founded the city, which was known to ancient Egyptians as Mennof-Ra. The patron god of Memphis, Ptah, was worshiped at the Temple of Ptah in Memphis. Saqqara, just west of Memphis, was a burial place for pharaohs of the Old Kingdom.

The Step Pyramid of the third-dynasty pharaoh, Djoser, with its six decreasing stone platforms, is the era's greatest monument. The fourth dynasty's pharaohs built Egypt's most impressive pyramids in Giza including the Great Pyramid of Cheops, also known as the Pyramid of Khufu, and the smaller pyramid of Chephren, also known as Khafre. Chephren, pharaoh of Egypt during the fourth dynasty, commanded a rock knoll be carved into the Giant Sphinx of Giza and given his own features. The later pyramid of Menkaure is also part of the Giza Plateau.

Statues from this period show idealized depictions of the pharaohs; they are portrayed as serene and majestic without human weakness. This style suited the Egyptians, who believed that their rulers were gods. Pharaohs were the sons of Ra, the sun god and first pharaoh. During the fifth and sixth dynasties, the religious power of the priests of Ra began to rival that of the pharaohs themselves. The monarchs built temples to Ra that outshone their own tombs.

Throughout the sixth dynasty, raids into Libya, Syria, and Palestine, as well as expeditions to Nubia,

The Great Pyramid

The core blocks for the Great Pyramid weighed as much as 200 tons each. They were found locally. Many of the thirty-ton granite facing-blocks were brought 500 miles (804 km) from Aswan by boat. All of these pieces were placed and joined with incredible accuracy. This was probably the work of a permanent staff of highly skilled workers, supported by unemployed peasants, or *fellahin*, during the flood season.

The Great Pyramid of Khufu (*center*), seen here with the Pyramids of Khafre (*right*) and Menkaure (*left*), is considered one of the seven wonders of the ancient world, though all the Egyptian pyramids in Giza are breathtaking works of architectural achievement. Each was built during the Old Kingdom (2686-2160 BC), often referred to as the great age of pyramids.

beyond Egypt in the south, and Sinai to the east, added to Egypt's wealth. Then the government weakened and Egypt broke into smaller units under the influence of weak rulers. Upper and Lower Egypt were once again separate.

The Middle Kingdom

By 2133 BC, the Upper Egyptian kings of Thebes had reunified Egypt. The twelfth dynasty moved the capital from Thebes to Ithet Tawy, near Memphis. They built a canal through the first cataract and the barrage across the Hawara Channel. This lowered the water level in the Fayyum and opened 16,803 acres (6,800 hec-tares) of land for farming. Many kings of the Middle Kingdom created public works. They viewed themselves as shepherds of the common people.

During this period, pyramids were fortresses. They were impassable both to tomb raiders and, according to Egyptian beliefs, evil spirits. One pharaoh built a 114-acre (46-ha) temple guarded by a maze. An intruder would enter through a web of passages filled with dead ends, death traps, sliding stones, and false chambers filled with worthless rubble.

By 1720 BC, Asiatic invaders had taken the eastern Delta around Avaris. These were the Hyksos, which is a Greek word for "rulers of foreign

The Egyptian settlement of workers' homes and their tombs *(above)*, founded between the eighteenth and twentieth dynasties, were once home to a community of workers who dug the graves in the Valley of the Kings. The settlement contained approximately seventy mud-brick structures, often with small cellars to store valuables. Because grave-digging was done secretly, the location of the workers' homes was never revealed. Even the food the workers ate was delivered to the restricted area. This archaeological site is located near the Valley of the Kings, west of the Nile River at Thebes.

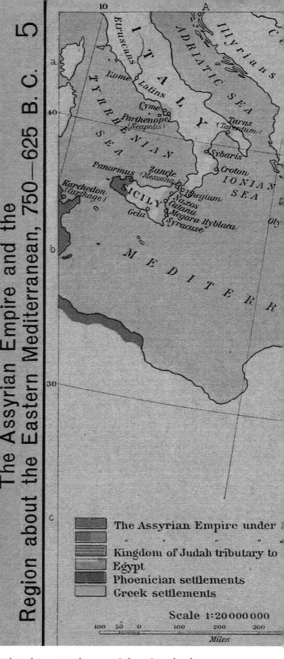

This historical map *(above)*, which shows the extent of ancient Egypt during the rise of the Assyrian Empire between 750 and 635 BC, was printed in 1923. Egypt's geographical relationship to the civilizations of the Greeks, Romans, Phoenicians, and Hebrews during this period is also indicated. An Egyptian worker, Sennedjem, is pictured with his wife Lyneferti *(inset)* farming a field in an image that was found inside their family tomb, located in a workers' settlement near the Valley of the Kings at Thebes.

lands." The Hyksos formed the fifteenth and sixteenth dynasties. They were great traders. During this period, Egyptian scarabs (carvings of sacred beetles) reached Knossos (on Crete) and Baghdad (in present-day Iraq). The Hyksos also introduced the horse-drawn chariot, the composite bow, and the vertical loom.

The seventeenth dynasty drove the Hyksos back to Palestine, took control of Nubia as far south as the second cataract (in present-day Sudan), and occupied Palestine and Syria north to the Euphrates River.

The New Kingdom

The eighteenth dynasty was the first of newly independent Egypt. Its campaigns brought great

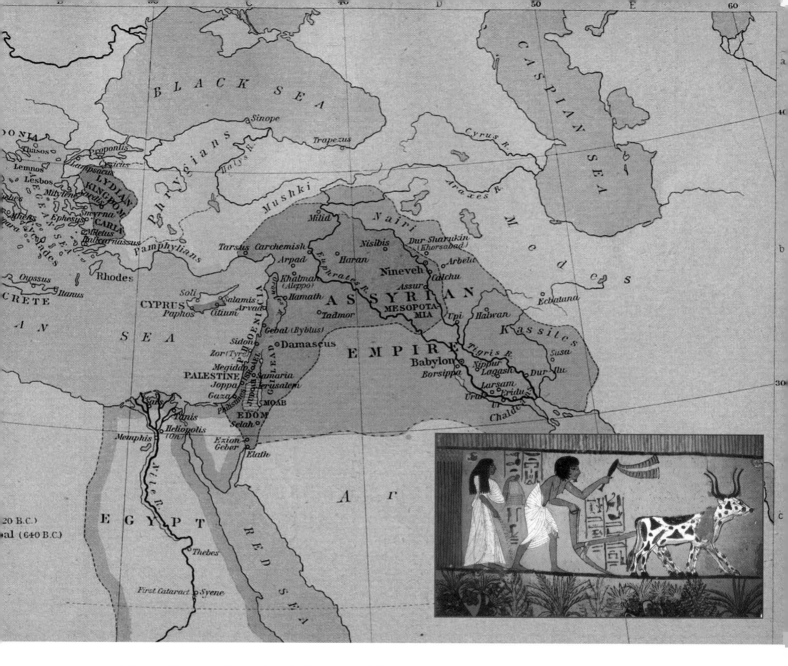

wealth to Egypt. Much of this wealth ended up in the hands of the priests of Amun. Egyptian mythology included many gods. Amun began as a minor deity of Thebes and eventually blended with the all-powerful sun god, Ra.

The power of Amun's priests threatened the throne. New cults developed to oppose it. The most dra-matic cult was that of Pharaoh Amenophis IV. He worshiped Aten, renamed himself Akhenaten ("he who serves Aten"), forbade worship of other gods, and closed their temples. The names of other gods were hastily hacked out of temple inscriptions.

Akhenaten was succeeded by his brother Tutankhamen in 1336 BC. Tutankhamen returned the capital to

Egyptian artists were extremely talented. They carved stone using a variety of sophisticated techniques, including bas-relief, like this carving of an Egyptian prisoner. Bas-relief is a stone-carving technique in which the figure projects from the background.

Memphis and restored the temples to their gods. In 1922, British archaeologist Howard Carter discovered Tutankhamen's rich burial tomb almost intact.

The nineteenth and twentieth dynasties built temples and monuments throughout Egypt, Nubia, and Palestine. The last great native pharaoh of Egypt was Ramses III. He crushed the Libyans early in his reign, and his people enjoyed great peace and prosperity. After his death, weaker leaders lost the colonies in Palestine. A series of Libyan and Nubian dynasties followed.

The Nubians placed their capital near the fourth cataract. In 760 BC, the Nubian ruler declared himself king of Upper and Lower Egypt. His successor captured Memphis. The Assyrians, who had long threatened Egypt, chose this point to invade. By 667 BC, they fully occupied the Delta.

The Egyptian Necho ruled Lower Egypt as an Assyrian vassal. His son, Psammetichus, reunited Egypt under the Assyrians. Meanwhile, the Assyrians fell to the Babylonians who fell to the Persians in 539 BC. In 525 BC, the Persians took Egypt. The twenty-seventh dynasty in Egypt was Persian. The Egyptians chafed under the Persians but were unable to drive them out. Persian rule finally ended when the Macedonian-born Greek conqueror Alexander the Great arrived in Egypt in 332 BC. The Egyptians hailed him as their deliverer from Persian dominance.

3 EGYPT UNDER GREECE, ROME, AND BYZANTIUM

During the so-called Ptolemaic period (332–30 BC), the Egyptians welcomed Alexander as a hero and made him a pharaoh in 332 BC. He accepted, founded Alexandria, and left to conquer the Persians. When Alexander died just nine years later in 323, Egypt passed to Ptolemy I, the son of one of Alexander's bodyguards. Under Ptolemy I, Egyptian culture blended with the Hellenistic culture of Greece.

One of the Greeks' most impressive achievements in Egypt was the city of Alexandria, which dominated the eastern Mediterranean coast for almost 700 years. Alexandria soon became even more important than Memphis. It was described during the first century BC by the geographer, Strabo, who wrote,

> "The whole city is criss-crossed with [wide] streets . . . magnificent public precincts and . . . royal palaces. The most beautiful building is the gymnasium . . . [but] there is also the Paneum, an artificially [created] height . . . ascended by a spiral stair. From the top, one has a panoramic view of the whole city lying below."

The first thing ancient travelers sailing into Alexandria saw was a long line of royal palaces

One of the seven wonders of the ancient world, Alexandria's great Pharos lighthouse guided ships for a thousand years before it was completely destroyed by earthquakes. Archaeologists now believe they have found thousands of stone fragments on the shallow floor of the Mediterranean harbor, originally blocks from the lighthouse that finally collapsed into the sea in 1341.

framed by soft green gardens. These lay at a northeast angle on the point of Lochias, which cradled the harbor on the east. Closer in, the high slim obelisks of Cleopatra's Needles marked the port.

One of the seven wonders of the ancient world was the great lighthouse of Pharos, which stood in one of Alexandria's two large harbors. The lighthouse rose more than 126 feet (38 meters) in three stories. Inside, the reflection of a small fire was magnified in order to be seen from a great distance out at sea.

Within the city were the famous Museum and Library of Alexandria. The Ptolemies encouraged learning. Ptolemy Philadelphus himself acquired 54,000 books from the Mediterranean area alone, as well as texts from India, Persia, Armenia, and Babylon. In the library, scholars translated the Old Testament into Greek and studied Euclid's geometry, as well as the most progressive medical and astronomical research of the time.

Alexandria remained an important city until the twelfth century AD. About that time, its channel to the Nile filled with silt and it lost access to the river system of Egypt.

The End of Ancient Egypt

Under the Greeks, Romans, and Byzantines, Egypt stretched from the Mediterranean in the north to the first cataract near present-day Aswan in the south. In the west, it ran into the Libyan Desert. In the northeast, it bordered the Arabian Desert from the Gulf of Suez to Rhinocoloura on the Mediterranean coast. In the southeast, it ended at the western coast of the Red Sea.

The Greeks improved irrigation and drainage. They planted new crops such as cotton and grapes.

The Library of Alexandria

The Library of Alexandria was one of the great monuments of the classical age. Two thousand years ago, its 700,000 scrolls were a nearly complete collection of world literature. Its destruction was a terrible tragedy.

According to the Greek historian Plutarch, in 48 BC, Caesar was fighting in Alexandria. To avoid being cut off from his fleet, he set fire to the dockyard and accidentally destroyed the library. In AD 391, a group of Christians ruined the Sarapeum, a branch of the library, and in 642, according to a twelfth-century source, Arabs heated the bathhouses of Alexandria for six months by burning the remaining scrolls.

Two thousand years later, the Arab world has built a new Library of Alexandria. Helped by major financial contributions from Iraq, Saudi Arabia, and the United Arab Emirates, Egypt's new library is a cylindrical building with an outer wall of unpolished Aswan granite, engraved with signs and letters from every known system of writing and houses books donated from all over the world.

Scholars converse in this undated illustration of the ancient library in Alexandria, a city that was once the center of a Hellenistic empire that spanned both Europe and Asia. The new Bibliotheca Alexandria opened in 2001 near where the ancient library once stood overlooking the Mediterranean Sea. The rounded futuristic aluminum and glass structure, which appears to rise from the earth at an angle that also allows it to act as a giant sundial, took twenty years to complete.

The three large areas of farmland—the Nile Valley, the Delta, and the Fayyum—may have been as much as 15,000 square miles (38,850 square kilometers) of farmable land.

The Romans absorbed the country into their empire after the death of Cleopatra, the last Ptolemy and Egypt's last pharaoh. The Romans loved the formality and magnificence

This map shows Egypt as a part of the Macedonian Empire before the death of Alexander the Great in 323 BC. Although Alexander established Alexandria in his own name, he died before the city was completed. The spread of Greek culture, however, continued to influence the region even after Alexander's death when the Ptolemy family began its reign over Egypt. The Ptolemaic period (323–30 BC) represented Alexandria's golden age and its rise as a cultural center of the world. Alexandria's grand palace, harbor, Pharos lighthouse, and library were all built during this time.

of Egypt and had even shipped twelve Egyptian obelisks back to Rome. Although the Romans respected the ancient culture of Egypt, Roman troops fought battles with Egyptians almost immediately. Leadership strategies changed as the Roman emperors governed Egypt from Rome, abolishing the Greek senate in Alexandria. Soon, fighting between Greeks and Romans began marking a troublesome beginning of Egypt's Christian era.

Still, the rise of Christianity after the death of Jesus Christ eroded the pagan culture of ancient Egypt. Jesus claimed to be the son of God and preached a new religion of peace and forgiveness. Fragments of the gospel of St. John, written in Coptic and found in Upper Egypt, testify to the spread of Christianity throughout Egypt. At first, the Romans, who, like the Egyptians, worshiped many gods, persecuted Jesus and his followers. Slowly, however, Christianity gained more and more Egyptian converts. Over time, Egypt's old gods were forgotten and its ancient traditions were lost.

Egypt is shown as a Roman province on this historical map of the eastern (Byzantine) half of the Roman Empire. The restoration and building that was started in Egypt during the reign of Alexander the Great and under the Ptolemies continued during Egypt's Roman Coptic period. It was also during this time when many of Egypt's ancient temples were converted to Christian churches and monasteries. This map was first printed in 1916 in an atlas entitled *East and West Through Fifteen Centuries*.

Coptic Egypt

The Egyptian Christians are called Coptics. The word "Coptic" comes from the Arabic term for Egyptian Christians, *al-Qubt*, which came from the Greek name for Egypt, *Aigyptos*.

According to Coptic tradition, St. Mark brought Christianity to Egypt in the first century AD. Most early converts were Jews or Greeks who were largely condemned for their beliefs. Some escaped by moving to the edge of the desert to live in isolation. One of these was St. Anthony. At the end of the third century, he founded a religious village in the desert.

There was much persecution of Christians in the fourth century, producing martyrs, or people who died for their religion. Their cause attracted more converts. By the fifth century, Christianity was popular even in the Byzantine capital

Many of Egypt's Coptic churches and monasteries remain unchanged from the time they were converted from earlier Egyptian temples or built from the remains of older structures. This semicircular vaulted apse, part of an early Egyptian Christian basilica, is one example of the beauty of Egypt's Roman period. The art and artifacts from Coptic Egypt were highly influenced by the culture of the ancient Greeks.

of Constantinople. When the Byzantine emperor Constantine made Christianity the official religion of the Roman Empire, even more Egyptians converted.

Although native Egyptian religions continued, they now had fewer followers. Temples lost their worshipers and many became Christian churches. The last, the Temple of Isis at Philae, closed in AD 527. This was also the site of the last hieroglyphic inscription in AD 394. As the Egyptians converted to Christianity, they ceased to use old Egyptian writing. They instead used the Greek alphabet with the addition of seven extra letters.

During the rule of Byzantine emperor Heraclius, the Persians invaded Alexandria. Twelve Persian soldiers disguised as fishermen rowed into the canal that circled the ancient city from the harbor side. They unlocked the Moon Gate, the northernmost boundary of Alexandria's main avenue, and ushered in the Persian army.

Heraclius's soldiers freed Egypt briefly but soon faced a greater danger. The Arab Muslims, then known to the Egyptians as Mohammedans, entered Egypt in 639 and attacked from the east. Arabs soon controlled the Middle East.

After the Arab conquest, freedom of worship lasted until the eleventh century when the Muslim caliph al-Hakim began to persecute Christians. The Coptic community soon dwindled, but some villages remained faithful. In Upper Egypt, Coptic was a living language until the sixteenth century. Today it is used only in the Coptic Church, to which 6 percent of Egyptians belong. It is the last living link to one of the languages of ancient Egypt.

4 THE ARAB INVASION

The Arab general 'Amr ibn al-As arrived in North Africa in AD 639, and led Arab armies into the region. Within six months, Arabs had conquered Egypt. The native Egyptians disliked the Byzantines and were happy with the change. The Arabs did not sack Egypt or enslave its people. The Arab ruler was known to be in favor of long-standing taxes, rather than the instantaneous spoils of war. He said, "In the name of God, the merciful, the compassionate, this is the amnesty granted to the people of Egypt, to their religion, their goods, their churches and crosses, their lands and waters, nothing of which shall be touched or seized from them." In return, the Egyptians paid a land tax when the Nile provided a bountiful harvest.

The Arabs moved the Egyptian capital from Alexandria to Fustat near Memphis, where the Mosque of 'Amr remains today. In time, the Arabs changed Egypt's official language from Coptic to Arabic. Native Egyptians were now forced to learn Arabic in order to keep their official positions in government. Egyptian currency was now minted in Damascus, Syria, the Arab capital. A postal service linked Fustat, which flourished as a center of trade, to the capital city. Slowly, Coptic-speaking Christian Egypt became Arabic-speaking Muslim Egypt.

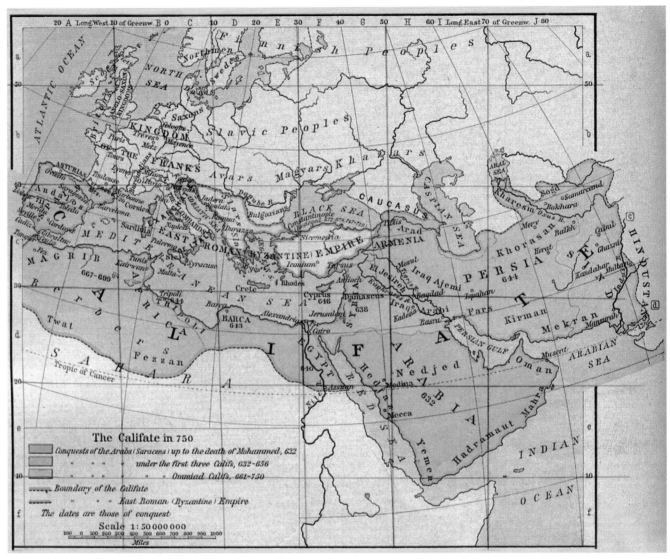

This historical map includes Egypt as part of the Arab Empire in AD 750. After Arab armies swept into North Africa in AD 639, Egypt surrendered within six months. It then became part of the 'Abbasid caliphate (AD 749–1258), joining an empire that included present-day Saudi Arabia, Yemen, Oman, the United Arab Emirates, Iraq, Iran, and portions of Syria and Turkey. Gradually, more and more Muslims settled in Egypt, setting the stage for the nation to become the Islamic country it is today.

In some ways, this was not a radical change. Both Christians and Muslims were monotheists, or believers in one god. Muslims followed the teachings of Muhammad, who claimed a messenger of God appeared to him near Mecca, in present-day Saudi Arabia. Muhammad taught people to forsake idols and nature spirits and worship the one true God, whom Muslims call Allah.

Muhammad admired the earlier monotheistic religions of Judaism and Christianity, and was the last in a line of prophets that included Abraham, Moses, and Jesus.

The Muslim Turks

Beginning in 834, Egypt was governed by Muslim Turks who seized Baghdad, the Arab capital (in present-day Iraq). In 868, Ahmad ibn Tulun took power and ran Egypt as an independent state. Under Tulun, Egypt expanded north into Syria. Trade and farming flourished and taxes dropped. When Tulun died, his government had great wealth. Tulun's successors were unable to hold Egypt against the Arab caliph, and soon it was folded back into the Arab Empire.

In 935, Egypt enjoyed another governor, Muhammad ibn Tughg al-Ikhshid of Damascus. Ikhshid and his successors encouraged Egyptian culture, and its people held festivals to celebrate the rise of the Nile. Egyptian *fellahin* (peasants) broke the dams to allow the river water to flood the fields in September. When the river receded, farmers rebuilt the dams and planted crops. During the festival,

Medieval Cairo

Between 1046 and 1049, a Persian traveler named Nasiri Khusrau visited Cairo. He guessed there were 20,000 dwellings in the city. Many were six stories high, surrounded by irrigated gardens. A mile away, in Fustat, buildings housed 350 people each. The sewers were deep and clean and serviced daily with lime. At night, lamps lit the streets. Wonderful wares were available in the markets: lustrous fabrics, fine carpets, and delicate pottery, some of it glazed to look metallic. Jewelers left their shops unlocked and no one stole from them.

Situated in the medieval sector of Cairo is the Qaitbay Mosque and Tomb, also known as the Qaitbay Madrassa, built between 1472 and 1474 by Sultan Qaitbay. Islamic art and architecture from the medieval period is often recognized by its elaborate calligraphy, geometric patterned designs, and unique and detailed architecture.

5 THE MAMLUKS AND THE OTTOMANS

The Mamluks ruled Egypt from 1250 to 1516. They were a class of male slaves trained as warriors. Adult Mamluks bought young slaves in the Russian Urals, Central Asia, the Caucasus Mountains, and later in Greece. They trained them to fight and ride on horseback, converted them to Islam, and taught them Arabic. At puberty, the boys were freed and given money and property to establish their own households.

Mamluk rule was foreign, but it made Egypt an independent kingdom and the center of the Mamluk Empire. The Mamluk era was a time of great art and architecture. Mamluk rulers, or sultans, built madrassas (Islamic schools) and monasteries. The artists and thinkers of Mamluk Egypt were famous throughout the Muslim world.

More important, the Mamluks offered Egypt military protection. Under General Baybars, they

The Italian monk Fra Mauro created this world map in the fifteenth century. At the time of its completion, it was considered among the world's greatest cartographic achievements. Because it preceded European discoveries about the relationships between the world's continents, however, it is now valued only for its beauty. Some of the map's images are of mythical beasts that were described to Mauro by Renaissance travelers. The map was created at the time between what was geographically unknown and the discoveries made during the age of exploration. Therefore, scholars consider it to be a transitional work of cartography.

...TO

esta arabia
a qual secon
...solin e de
...la. et bala
...ca de piume
...quarti colori
...resta. et circa
...color aureo. e.
...a el resto dele suer
...o de color pupure
...e altri ifiniti color.

...SERTO

...BIA
...DESER
...TA

...chu muor q̃sti
...rami de eu
...frates.

...meldeni

...ziabar

...chalaturo
...arabe

ainoit

ndie

abaa

madi

coidia

batasur

fonte

eltoz

eltorexi

pozo de
moyses

castel de
cozon

barasuis

masser
ouer el
chayro

babilonia

Nota chel sono d
...uno superio
qui son christiani
negri. el toro en
ferto egli si son
bruchi. e dai cha
...ero su u̓ra gra
...cuser ouer mia 400
...cuser e̓ na asia et
...superiore

zafrano

mons dimas TEBAIDA

badaragie

per questa ualle
se tien che
passase el populo
de israel

Egypto
supior

EGYPTo

aorā

olch

ASIA

ARABIA
PETREA

Gynay.

Questo mo̅fi dito
ancora oreb. çoe i q̃
la pte che moyses
receuete la leçe.

hache

Sel parera ad algun che io
no̅ habi ben posto babilo
nia per hauerla descripta
sopra tygris e non eufra
tes come scriueno li au
tori. piaquali prima co̅
desegnositerar q̃sto. e dapoi do
madi queli hano ue
duto a dochio. eintenderano
che io no̅ me parto dala
uerita.

Quel che sono experti
supli sca in questa co̅ u̓ mez
e palestina e galilea gli che
io no̅ meto. çoe el fiume
iordā. el mar tyberia
dis. el mar morto. et
altri luogi iq̅l eu u̓a
son no̅ se hano
possudo mete

deserto

laris
deserto

PALES
TINA

gaçara

elmeso
...el
el mino
...dmie

 menenit

IUDEA
SIRIA

capho

DESERTO
o

EUFRA
TES

SIRIA

Asiria
dama
...ci

PALE
STINA

HIERVSA
LEN e imezo de la tera
habitabile. secto la ia̅magine
de la tera habitabile. le
ch̅ e çoe la logem
dine da la sua piu or
...retal. ma poi la
per de piu occi
...etal. e piu halt
...apo g̅ euiops
...ghe imezo an
...cora secoto la lon

MA. EGYPTIA

El nilo come̅ça cresce
solsticio estinal. pas
et i̅ugine se afferma
come̅çar a crescer
e egripto una lan̅c

mordi

Io ho lassato am
plissimi deseg̅ni
de tute quelle p
te. çoe armeni
a. mesopotamia.
siria. capadocia.
cilicia. paphylia
...licia. asia spa menor

defended Egypt from the eastern Mongols. In 1258, the Mongol leader Hülagü, grandson of Genghis Khan, destroyed Baghdad, the Arab capital. Then he moved west into Syria. Baybars defeated him in battle and became sultan of Egypt. He was the first of the Bahri (river) Mamluk rulers, so named because his soldiers lived along the Nile.

Baybars organized a fair and diplomatic government. He reorganized the Egyptian army, strengthened Egypt's fortification and canals, and improved its harbors. As a result of this efficiency, Egypt prospered and even benefited from a postal system that could carry a letter from Cairo to Damasco in a week. After Baybars conquered Syria, his empire stretched to the Taurus Mountains.

One of Baybars's successors was General Qalawun. Qalawun built Egypt's first hospital, a place where patients were treated for free. In some wards, musicians played soothing music. Qalawun also built a mosque that showed the beauty and complexity of Mamluk design. Qalawun's dynasty ruled for a century, Egypt's period of greatest peace and prosperity.

Egypt's fortunes changed with the Black Death, a plague that appeared around 1348. It killed one-third of Egypt's population in eighteen attacks that occurred between 1348 and 1513. Because there was no one to farm the land, the Mamluks fell into debt. The Bahris lost control of the government and the Burgi Mamluks replaced them.

The Burgi Mamluks

The Burgis ruled from 1382 to 1517. At first, they struggled. Plague and bad harvests had driven the people into poverty. Hungry farmers had turned to robbery, making trade roads too dangerous for merchants and further draining Egypt's economy. Meanwhile, the Mamluks were fighting expensive wars in Syria and Anatolia (present-day Turkey) and needed to support their army. To do so, they taxed the Egyptian people.

In 1468, Sultan Qaitbay took power. He rebuilt the country; lowered taxes; built roads, bridges, mosques, and schools; and restored Egypt's monuments. His Fort Qaitbay still stands on the site of the old Pharos lighthouse in Alexandria.

Egypt had just begun to prosper again when, in 1492, another plague arrived. In Cairo, it killed 12,000 people a day. When Qaitbay died in 1496, the country was in chaos. In 1501, the last Mamluk sultan, Qansuh al-Ghuri, took the throne.

Meanwhile, the Ottoman Turks had grown more powerful. Their land now stretched to the Mamluks' northern border. The Ottoman sultan

This photograph, taken in 1910, shows the Northern Cemetery and Mosque Complex in Cairo, Egypt, which was reserved for Mamluks. Built between 1472 and 1474 during the reign of Mamluk sultan Qaitbay, the cemetery is now commonly called the "city of the dead."

took Syria, crushed the Persians, and turned on the Mamluks.

Al-Ghuri, who was then in his seventies, rode to battle in May 1516. The Ottomans defeated him north of Aleppo, Syria. The Mamluks had expected mounted hand-to-hand combat, but the Ottomans instead destroyed them with gunfire. The Mamluks were angry and disgusted at this battle, which they believed was won without honor, while the Ottomans laughed at the idea of a fair fight. In 1517, the Ottomans marched into Cairo and made a Mamluk traitor their viceroy. Cairo became a province of a new Muslim empire centered in Constantinople (present-day Istanbul).

Egypt remained an Ottoman province until 1914, sharing with the Turks the religion of Islam, but not language or ethnicity. Both the Egyptians and the remaining Mamluks wanted independence.

The Ottomans

In 1522, Egypt exploded in public revolt. To control it, the Ottoman

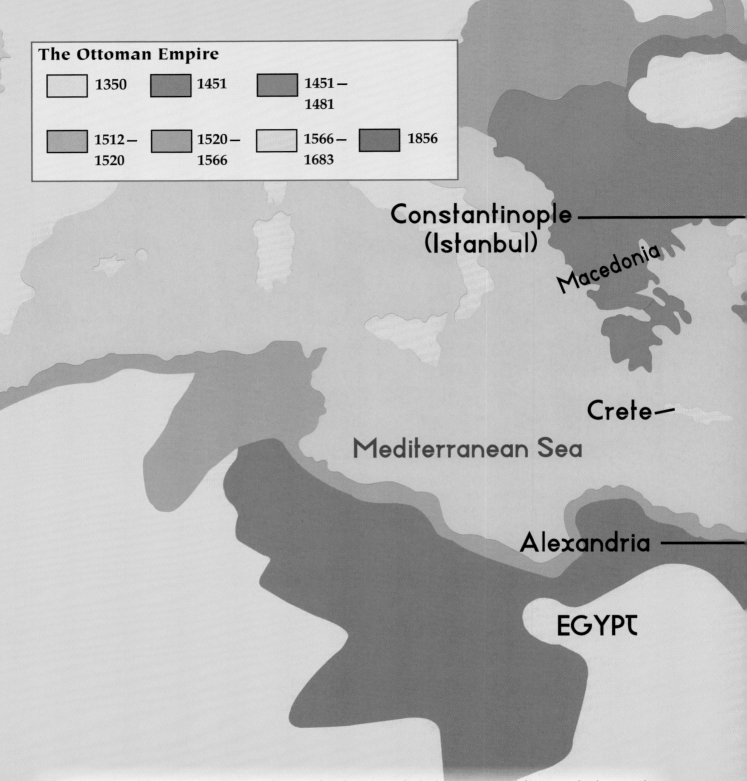

The Ottoman Empire

- 1350
- 1451
- 1451–1481
- 1512–1520
- 1520–1566
- 1566–1683
- 1856

Constantinople (Istanbul)

Macedonia

Crete

Mediterranean Sea

Alexandria

EGYPT

The expansion of the Ottoman Empire is illustrated in this map, which shows its growth between the fourteenth and nineteenth centuries. The Ottoman Empire was strengthened by the migration of Turks into the Arab Empire during the 'Abbasid period. Ottoman Turks converted to Islam and entered the region as Mamluks, creating larger and more powerful Arab armies. By the tenth century, a newer generation of free Turks gained control of the Arab government, which had been considerably weakened by earlier Mongol invaders. Soon the Turks gained enough power to overthrow the Arabs, absorbing Egypt between 1512 and 1520, and gradually expanding their empire until the nineteenth century.

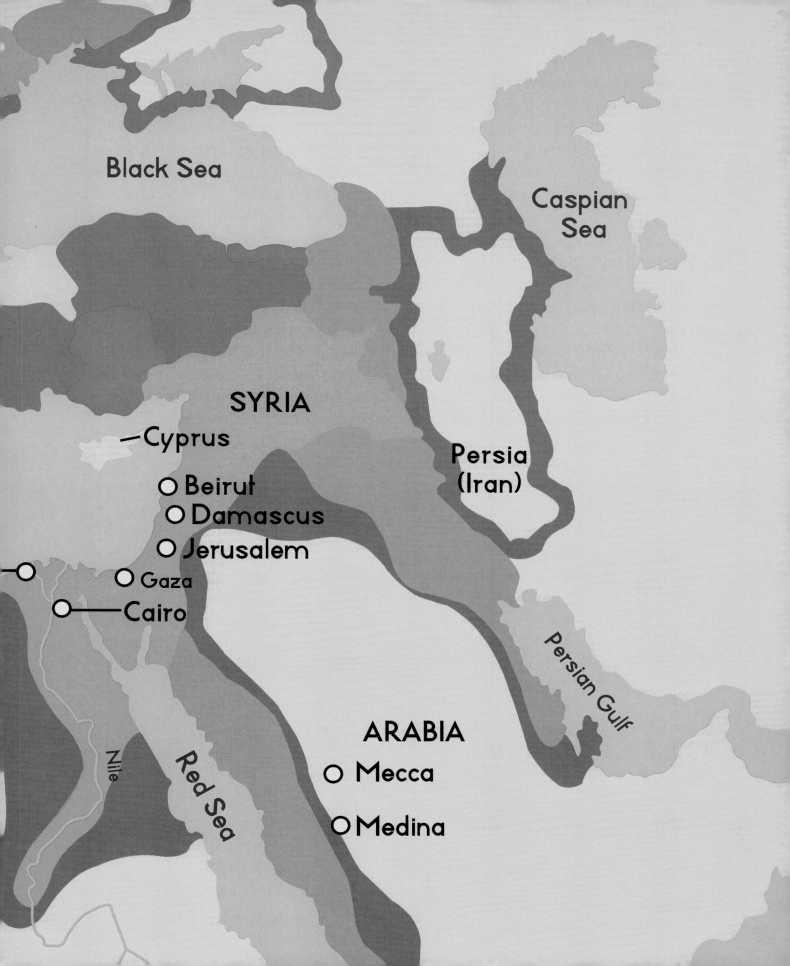

sultan cut the territory into fourteen provinces, each with a governor, known as a *pasha*, who answered to the Ottoman viceroy, or *wali*, in Cairo. Four times a week, the wali held a council, or *diwan*, to discuss the needs of the people.

The first sixty years of Ottoman rule were peaceful until the European invasions of the Americas created a flow of inexpensive silver that upset the gold-silver exchange. The value of Ottoman money dropped. Soldiers could no longer live on their salaries.

Underpaid Ottoman soldiers often protected wealthy artists and craftsmen for money. Sometimes they married artists' daughters. They had Egyptian children who grew up to be soldiers. This opened the Ottoman army to native Egyptians for the first time.

Late in the sixteenth century, Ottoman soldiers in Egypt rebelled to protest their wages. In 1609, a group of Mamluk soldiers who fought within the Ottoman army led a rebellion so violent that the Ottomans could barely contain it. They feared the Mamluks would try to retake the region and crush them.

More than a century later, in 1768, the Mamluk Ali Bey al-Kabir aka Bulut Kapan did try to retake Egypt. He wanted to make Egypt a free empire as Saladin and Tulun had done before. Ali Bey took charge of all fourteen provinces and bought guns and armed ships from the Russians. He might have won, but his second-in-command betrayed him. Ali Bey escaped to the desert where he was captured in 1773.

The Mamluks continued to govern, but they could not fight free of the Ottomans. Worse, the people hated them. The Egyptians were overtaxed and dissatisfied. The Nile did not rise high enough for good harvests. Starving fellahin walked in from the country to fall dead in city streets. The abandoned farmland could not produce food. The people grew desperate and staged revolts.

6 NAPOLÉON AND EGYPTOLOGY

By the late eighteenth century, the Ottomans could no longer control the angry Egyptians, so they turned to Europe for assistance. In 1798, the French general Napoléon Bonaparte sailed into Alexandria. Soon he occupied the city and overwhelmed the Mamluks, who fled east to Gaza and south to Upper Egypt.

Napoléon marched on to Cairo where he fought and won the Battle of the Pyramids. His intention was not simply to put down the rebellion, but to make Egypt a province of France. The betrayed Ottomans turned to the British. The British attacked and sank the French fleet in the Bay of Abuqir. Stranded inland, Napoléon found he could not control the whole country. Eleven months after taking Alexandria, he abandoned his men and returned to France.

The Birth of Egyptology

The most interesting part of Napoléon's arrival in Egypt was not related to the country's invasion. Napoléon was most fascinated by the monuments of ancient Egypt. The fifty scientists and scholars who traveled with his army, in fact, laid much of the foundation for the new science of Egyptology.

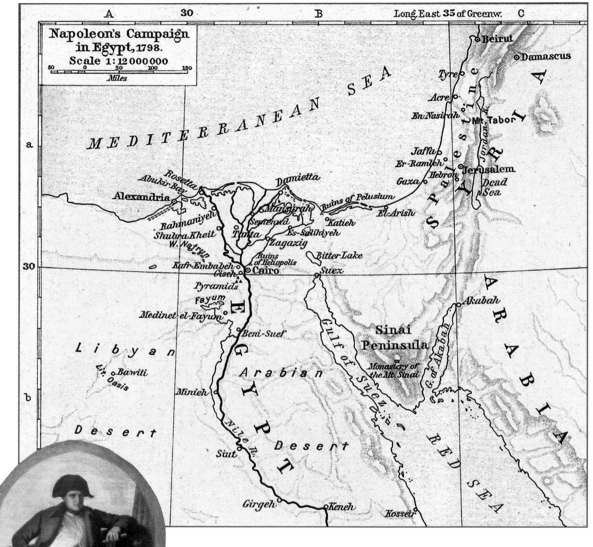

Napoleon's Campaign in Egypt, 1798.
Scale 1:12 000 000
Miles

Napoléon Bonaparte's campaign into Egypt is shown in this historic map (above). When Napoléon (left) led his armies into Alexandria, he told his soldiers to respect Muslims and the Islamic rituals that guided their lives. "People of Egypt," he said in 1798, "you will be told by our enemies, that I [have] come to destroy your religion. Believe them not. Tell them [instead] that I [have] come to restore your rights, punish your usurpers, and raise the true voice of Mahomet [Muhammad]." After brief victories over the Mamluks in Alexandria and Cairo, Napoléon returned to France defeated by 1801.

One of Napoléon's scholars was Dominique-Vivant Denon. Denon traveled into Upper Egypt and made careful sketches of the grand statues and immense ruins that appeared around every bend in the Nile. These were published as the Déscription de l'Egypte in 1809.

Europe's intellectuals, familiar with ancient Greece and Rome, were thrilled by this mysterious ancient culture, though none could translate the Egyptians' hieroglyphic script.

In 1799, one of Napoléon's engineers found the Rosetta Stone, which later became the key to unlocking the ancient alphabet. This was a large slab of black basalt dug out of a trench at Rosetta, near Alexandria. It was carved with text in three writing systems. In 1822, the French scholar Jean François Champollion guessed that the Greek on the stone, which he could read, was the same language as the hieroglyphics. This enabled him to translate the hieroglyphic alphabet. In 1828, he led an expedition to study inscriptions on statues, tombs, and temples.

Soon, archaeologists like Howard Carter, who located and opened the tomb of Tutankhamen, were traveling to Egypt to study ancient art

This is a detail of a modern replica of the famous Egyptian Rosetta Stone. The black basalt stone, world famous by 1822, was decoded by a French scholar named Jean François Champollion after he assumed that the Greek language on the stone was a direct translation of two other systems of writing, hieroglyphic and demotic. Because of Champollion's theory, hieroglyphs became accessible for the first time to contemporary scholars.

British archaeologist and Egyptologist Howard Carter (*center*) can be seen in this 1922 photograph inside the tomb of the Egyptian boy king Tutankhamen. At the time of its discovery, the ancient tomb was complete with priceless and beautiful artifacts that had not been exposed since approximately 1300 BC. Carter's other discoveries, though lesser known, include the tombs of the Pharaoh Thutmose IV and Queen Hatshepsut.

and architecture. They found temples, tombs, furniture, mummified remains, and papyrus documents. They also found artifacts from daily life such as toys, clothing, and drinking vessels. Slowly, they pieced together a detailed portrait of a people wholly lost to the modern world.

There were two main reasons for their discoveries. One was that ancient Egyptians, particularly royalty, carried the necessities and luxuries of their daily lives into their tombs. They decorated these tombs with everyday scenes of the court, the city, and the farmland fringing the Nile.

The second was the climate. Egypt's dry desert air safeguarded the bodies and belongings of the ancient Egyptians, items they hoped would prove useful in their next life. This "afterlife" turned out to be fame and preservation in the museums of a later world.

7 EGYPT BECOMES A NATION

The Ottomans threw the French out of Egypt in 1801. The Mamluks expected to return to power, but the Egyptians did not want them. Five hundred years earlier, the Egyptians accepted Mamluk rule because the Mamluks could protect them. After the French invasion, this was no longer true.

During his brief time in Egypt, Napoléon organized the religious leaders, or *ulama*, into *diwans*. These councils spoke with the voice of the whole Egyptian population. They decided to find Egypt a ruler who would care about the country.

Soon they met Muhammad Ali. Ali was a Turkish-speaking Muslim who led the Albanian wing of the Ottoman army. He told the ulama the Egyptians deserved better. Their country was rich in land and workers. With a fair and wise governor, Egypt would be peaceful and prosperous. The ulama offered to make Ali governor if he obeyed the will of the people.

Ali agreed to their terms, and the ulama led the people of Cairo in a revolt against the Ottoman government. They declared Muhammad Ali governor of Egypt. The Ottoman sultan agreed to the people's demands. Muhammad Ali took office in 1805. He spent the first six years crushing the Mamluks out of existence. His rule lasted until 1848 and his dynasty governed until 1952.

Industrialization

Ali recognized that as long as Egypt was a country of farmers, it would need to trade for certain goods. Only industry could make it a self-sufficient country. If Egypt could manufacture its own fabrics and weapons, it would not need to spend money abroad. Ali also wanted to be able to defend Egypt. His new factories made rifles, muskets, cannons, and pistols.

Ali's army conquered the area of modern Saudi Arabia and Sudan. Soon, Ali had too much territory to control with his soldiers. He could not afford to pay mercenaries, or soldiers-for-hire, like the Mamluks. Contacts in the French army suggested he draft Egyptian fellahin. This was a brand-new idea. Egyptian soldiers were not peasants; they belonged to a special warrior class. Ali followed the advice and raised the size of the army to 100,000 men.

Ali's decision led to a surprising social advance for Egypt. The new native Egyptian soldiers needed an education. Ali opened schools across the country to train soldiers, engineers, doctors, and veterinari-

Muhammad Ali, pasha of Egypt from 1806 until 1848, is depicted here in a nineteenth-century painting by British artist David Wilke. Ali helped modernize and industrialize Egypt, especially Cairo. His imperialistic ideas about extending Egypt's borders into Sudan, Arabia, and Syria, however, created conflicts with Great Britain and the Ottoman Empire.

ans. Students went abroad to learn new technologies and sciences and brought that knowledge back to Egypt.

These reforms cost money. Egypt began to export cotton, sugarcane, indigo, and flax. Farming grew more efficient. In earlier times, fellahin

This historic map of Africa, which shows Sudan as Egyptian territory, was printed in 1885 and published by the Scottish Geographical Society. The British had an ongoing interest in Egyptian affairs and security throughout the nineteenth century. This was especially true since the building of the Suez Canal in 1869 had made British trading in the region more profitable. Concerned that other nations had also set their sights on the Nile River, Egyptian-financed British forces repeatedly gained control of Sudan, and subsequently the Nile River, during the 1880s and 1890s.

worked about half the year. While the land was underwater, they became artisans who crafted leather or metal, or they relaxed. Now they planted according to a government schedule that took twice as much time. Any remaining days were spent digging ditches and clearing silt from canals.

This crunch occurred because there were fewer fellahin to do the work. Many now had industrial jobs in the city or had gone to join the army. Ali's soldiers fought in the Hijaz, Sudan, Crete, Cyprus, Morea, and Syria. Ali wanted Mediterranean colonies to control sea commerce and land colonies to control trade routes.

Ali's Egypt was the strongest military power in the Middle East. This threatened the Ottomans. War broke out and the Egyptians defeated the Ottomans at the Battle of Nizip in 1839. The Ottomans turned to the British. The British forced Ali out of Syria. Egypt, which had teetered on the brink of becoming a great empire, was again reduced to a province.

Still, Ali offered something greater to Egyptians than treasure or territory. He gave the Egyptians national pride. His army defeated the Ottomans as

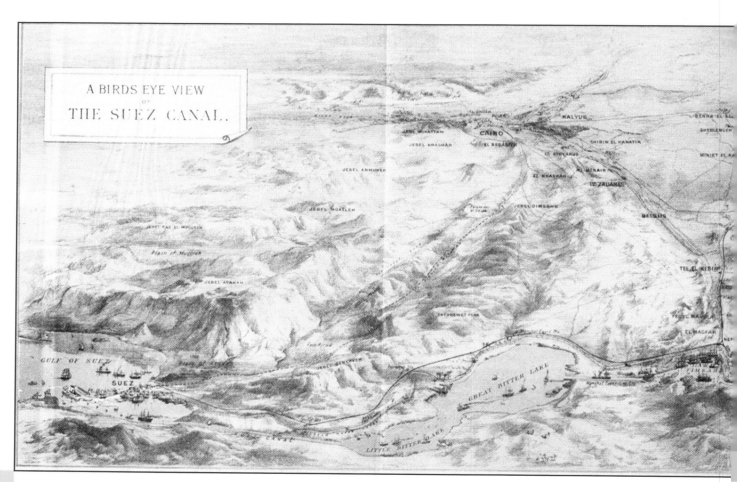

Egyptians fighting for Egypt. His schools provided education and opportunity; his industries led toward economic independence. The farming program introduced so many new plants that today, most of Egypt's fruit and vegetable crops originated from this period.

The Suez Canal

Muhammad Ali's successors followed in his nationalist footsteps. His son, Said, contracted the French to build the Suez Canal to connect the Mediterranean with the Red Sea in 1869. His grandson, Ismail, dug so many irrigation canals that the land could now produce two or three crops a year. Ismail also built roads, bridges, and lighthouses. Eventually these projects drove Egypt into debt. First he sold his share of the Suez Canal. This lost Egypt the money the canal provided from increased trading. Subsequently, Ismail had to liquidate his personal estates and accept British and French ministers in his cabinet. Then Ismail asked Europe for help.

Britain was delighted to take charge of the canal. This opened the door to foreign exploitation. Non-Egyptians moved into the country

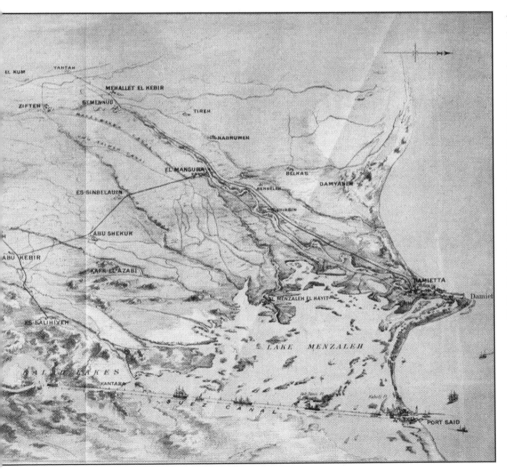

This map shows a view of Cairo and the Suez Canal, which is the world's largest canal without locks. The canal opened on November 17, 1869, and has since been an important trade and communication link between the Mediterranean and Red Seas. It was designed and financed by the French to allow for improved trading between European and Middle Eastern nations. It has also been a source of conflict for the Egyptians. This led to the Suez Crisis in 1956, when the Egyptians fought to establish control over the canal for more than eighty years. Pressure from the United States, the United Nations, and the Soviet Union ended the Suez Crisis by forcing a full restoration of Egyptian independence.

Egypt and Sinai are visible in this map of Egyptian territories from 1900. Although Egyptians longed for independence, Egypt's changing and unstable economy, which had become weak and impoverished during the early part of the twentieth century, created the need for foreign assistance from France and Great Britain.

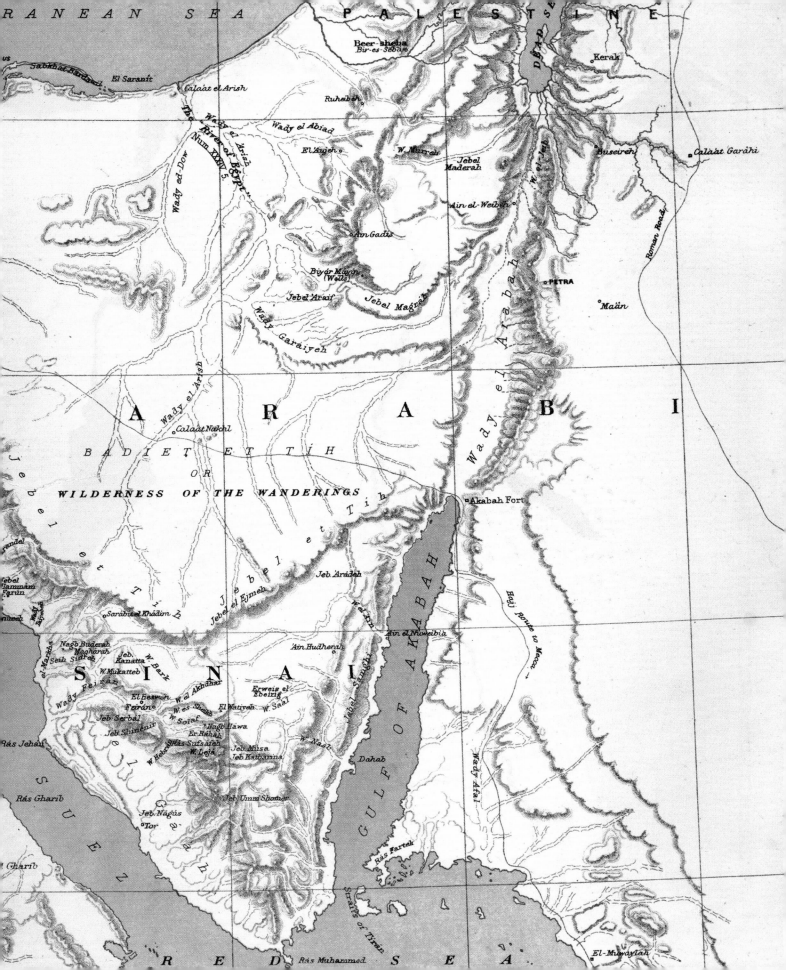

This cartoon exaggerates British dominance in Egypt during the late 1800s and early 1900s. The last Egyptian Ottoman khedive (governor or ruler), Abbas II, who ruled from 1892 until 1914, is seen under the foot of a British army officer. Although Abbas pushed toward Egypt's independence, occupying British forces ignored his efforts.

One night, a drunken Greek stabbed an Arab shepherd. The city exploded. People fought in the streets and fired guns from their windows. Parts of the city were in flames. The British landed and sent troops down the Suez Canal. They surrounded and crushed the Egyptians. To Tewfik's surprise, instead of ending the conflict and leaving, the British continued to occupy Egypt.

and lived without paying taxes. Native Egyptians paid taxes to support not only themselves but also many foreigners. The injustice drove them to revolt. Wealthy landowners, student intellectuals, and army officers all joined together under the slogan "Egypt for the Egyptians."

Egypt's ruler and son of Ismail, Muhammad Tewfik, appointed in 1879, turned to Europe for assistance. British and French ships anchored at Alexandria. Tension was very high.

The Egyptian people were horrified by their failure. The nationalists lay quiet for ten years. Secular (nonreligious) nationalism grew stronger between 1890 and 1906 from Egypt's enormous prosperity, derived from cotton harvests. Then, Tewfik's sixteen-year-old son, Abbas Hilmi, resolved to free Egypt from the British. With his help, young Egyptian students and nationalists organized strikes and demonstrations calling for Egyptian independence.

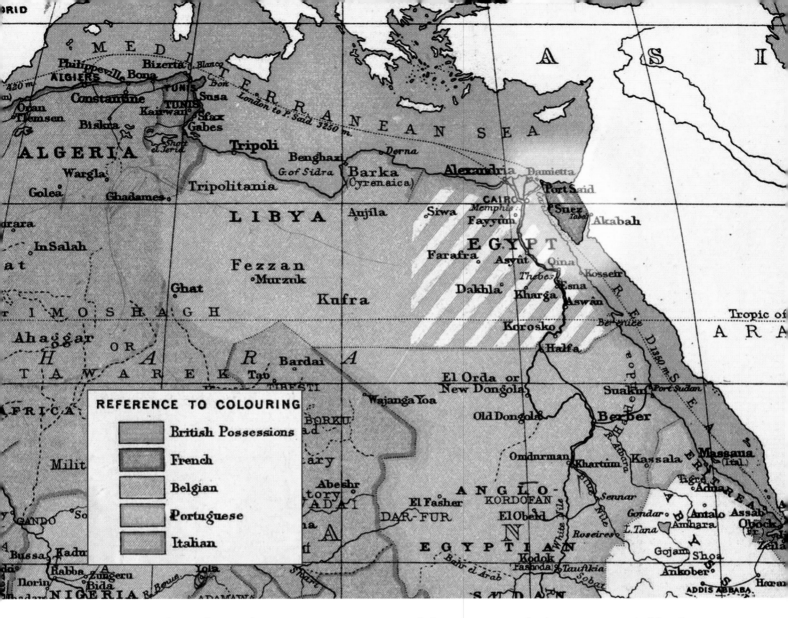

This historical British map designates areas in Egypt and the Sinai Peninsula that were occupied by the British beginning in 1936. Although both Britain and France had interests in Egypt during the 1800s and 1900s, it was the British who ultimately controlled the area around the Suez Canal, as determined by provisions in the Anglo-Egyptian treaty. Despite an urgency by Egyptian leaders for the British to withdraw from the "Canal Zone," they maintained their forces there until 1956.

The British ignored this. They had no intention of leaving Egypt. Britain needed Egypt's raw materials for its own industry. In 1902, the British dammed the Nile at Aswan to increase farmable land and profits.

The Egyptians were unhappy with the British presence. Britain agreed to discuss Egypt's independence after World War I (1914–1918). By 1922, it offered Egypt partial sovereignty. The Egyptians governed themselves, but British soldiers remained in a small territory dubbed the "Canal Zone" near the Suez Canal.

8 THE ARAB REPUBLIC OF EGYPT

*KEY TO GOVERNORATES
IN NILE DELTA*

Governorate	Capital
1 AD DAQAHLĪYAH	Al Manşūrah
2 AL BUHAYRAH	Damanhūr
3 AL GHARBĪYAH	Tanţā
4 AL ISKANDARIYYAH	Al Iskandariyyah (Alexandria)
5 AL ISMĀ'ĪLĪYYAH	Al Ismā'īlīyyah
6 AL MNŪFĪYAH	Shibīn Al Kawm
7 AL QĀHIRAH	Al Qāhirah (Cairo)
8 AL QALYŪBĪYAH	Banhā
9 ASH SHARQĪYAH	Az Zaqāzīq
10 BŪR SA'ĪD	Būr Sa'īd (Port Said)
11 DUMYĀŢ	Dumyāţ
12 KAFR ASH SHAYKH	Kafr ash Shaykh

✪	National capital
◉	Governorate capital
○	Town, village
✈	Major airport
•	Cistern, spring, well
----·----·	International boundary
--·--·--	Governorate boundary
——	Dual highway

Egypt's new semi-independent government was controlled by two men—a prime minister and a king. Prime Minister Saad Zaghlul was from an agricultural background and spoke for the people. King Fuad was raised abroad and barely spoke Arabic. He wanted a traditional monarchy. Zaghlul worked to improve the lives of average Egyptians. When Zaghlul died in 1927, his constitutional Wafd (delegation) government died with him. Fuad's new government favored rich landowners. Two percent of the people owned half the land.

Egypt continued to tolerate and support the British soldiers in the Canal Zone. Between World War I and World War II, Egypt suffered an economic depression. Wages dropped and food prices rose. The Egyptian people, struggling and starving, watched as their government

Egypt is seen in this contemporary map from the United States Central Intelligence Agency (CIA). The British, who occupied Egypt and made the country an official British colony from 1882 until 1923, were largely interested in utilizing Egypt's Suez Canal. British access to and control over the Suez Canal made trading between Great Britain and India safer and more efficient. Facing increased opposition from growing Egyptian nationalists pushing for Egypt's independence, Great Britain declared Egypt an official British protectorate in 1914.

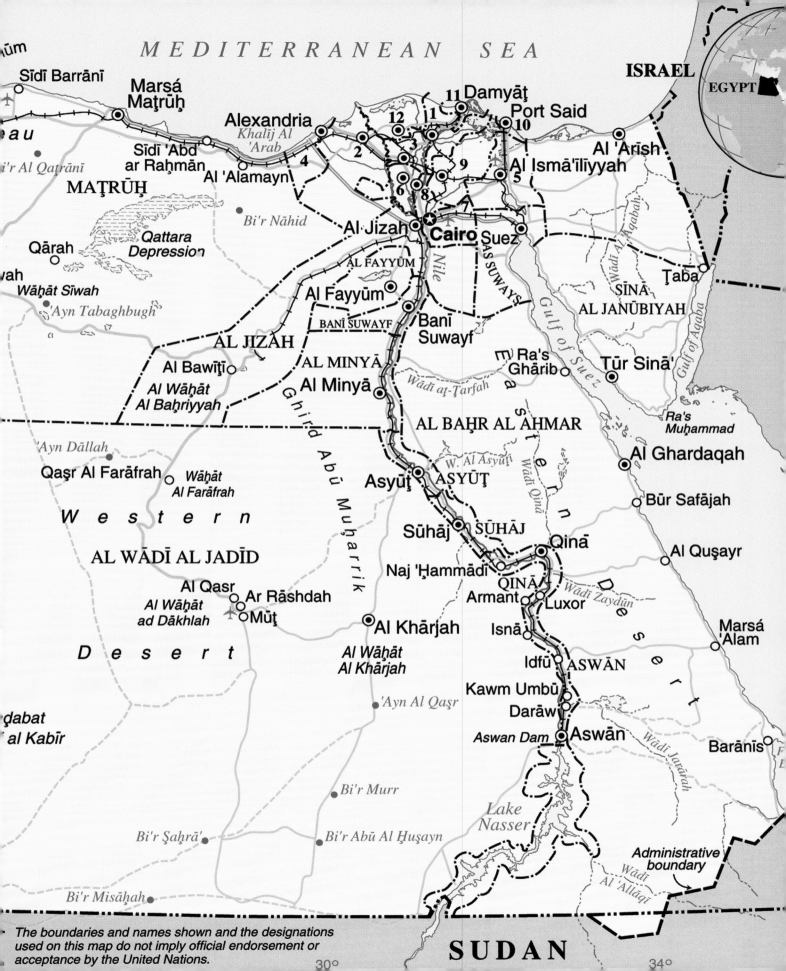

MEDITERRANEAN SEA

ISRAEL

EGYPT

Sīdī Barrānī
Marsá Maṭrūḥ
Sīdī 'Abd ar Raḥmān
Al 'Alamayn
MAṬRŪḤ

Alexandria
Khalīj Al 'Arab

11 Damyāṭ
Port Said
12
1
3
10
9
Al Ismā'īlīyyah
5
Al 'Arīsh

Qārah
Bi'r Al Qaṭrānī
Bi'r Nāhid
Qattara Depression
Wāḥāt Sīwah
'Ayn Tabaghbugh

2
4
6
8

Al Jizah
Cairo
Suez

AS SUWAYS

SĪNĀ AL JANŪBIYAH

Wādī Al 'Aqabah

Ṭaba

Qārah

AL FAYYŪM
Al Fayyūm
BANĪ SUWAYF
Bani Suwayf

Nile

Gulf of Suez

Gulf of Aqaba

Ra's Ghārib
Ṭūr Sīnā'

AL JIZAH

AL MINYĀ
Al Minyā

Wādī aṭ-Ṭarfah

Ra's Muḥammad

Al Bawīṭī
Al Wāḥāt Al Baḥriyyah

Ghird Abū Muḥarrik

AL BAḤR AL AḤMAR

W. Al Asyūṭī

Al Ghardaqah

'Ayn Dāllah
Qaṣr Al Farāfrah
Wāḥāt Al Farāfrah

Asyūṭ
ASYŪṬ

Wādī Qinā

Būr Safājah

Western

AL WĀDĪ AL JADĪD

Sūhāj
SŪHĀJ

Al Qasr
Ar Rāshdah
Al Wāḥāt ad Dākhlah
Muṭ

Naj 'Ḥammādī
Qinā
QINĀ

Wādī Zaydūn

Al Quṣayr

Eastern Desert

Al Khārjah

Al Wāḥāt Al Khārjah

Armant
Luxor
Isnā

Marsá 'Alam

Desert

'Ayn Al Qaṣr

Idfū
Kawm Umbū
Darāw

ASWĀN

ḍabat al Kabīr

Aswan Dam
Aswān

Wādī Jarārah

Barānīs

Bi'r Murr

Lake Nasser

Bi'r Şaḥrā'
Bi'r Abū Al Ḥusayn

Administrative boundary

Wādī Al 'Allāqī

Bi'r Misāḥah

SUDAN

30°   34°

housed and fed British soldiers. Many Egyptians were Muslims who did not drink alcohol, which is forbidden in Islam. During the early years of World War II (1939–1945), Egyptians with hungry children watched with disgust as British officers drank alcohol in expensive clubs.

When the war ended, Egypt insisted the British leave for good. On July 23, 1952, a group of young Egyptian officers led by Gamal Abdel Nasser overthrew the government. They called themselves the Free Officers, dethroned Fuad's son, Faruq, in a coup, and dismantled the British-backed government. One year later, 1953, Egypt became the Arab Republic of Egypt.

Decolonization

When Nasser became president, Egypt was one of many countries that had just rid itself of an imperial power like Britain. Many African, Middle Eastern, and Asian countries were pushing out the Western powers that had colonized them. This was called decolonization. These countries, which had less industry and money than their European colonizers, were "developing" countries. Nasser found allies among such leaders of the developing world as President Tito of Yugoslavia, Pandit Nehru of India, and President Sukarno of Indonesia.

Nasser

Nasser became president of Egypt in 1956, after having been prime minister and virtual dictator since 1954. He wanted to develop the country into a world power. He planned the Aswan High Dam project to double Egypt's farmable land and to create hydroelectric power for industry. After failing to receive

Hailed by Egyptian nationalists, Egyptian president Gamal Abdel Nasser, seen here in 1964, led a successful bloodless coup to challenge the British-controlled Egyptian government in 1952. Within two years, he took full control over Egypt, where he remained in power for eighteen years until he died suddenly in 1970.

the money he expected from the United States, Nasser seized the Suez Canal from British control and used its income to pay for the dam. The canal was on Egyptian soil, but it was a run by a French company and used by the British. France and Britain tried to bargain with Nasser, but after he was insulted by the British prime minister, Nasser called off negotiations.

With the help of Israel, Britain and France attacked Egypt. The United States and the Union of Soviet Socialist Republics (U.S.S.R.) stopped the fighting. The Egyptians lost many more soldiers than their attackers, but for them, the battle was a victory. They had survived war with three countries and kept their valuable canal. Nasser's popularity increased. He stood for Arab unity and independence.

The Syrians particularly admired Nasser. Egypt and Syria shared certain ideas. One of these ideas was that the newly created state of Israel had no place in the Arab world. In 1948, at the end of the British occupation of Palestine, Israel became an independent Jewish nation. Many Arabs felt the Holy Land of Jerusalem belonged to Muslims, not Jews. The surrounding Arab countries, including Egypt, declared war on the new Jewish nation. Egypt

was in no shape to wage war, and the Israelis defended themselves easily. Although peace was restored in the region, hostility remained.

Eighteen years later, in 1966, Egypt and Syria formed a "defensive" alliance against Israel. On June 5, 1967, Israel struck first and destroyed Egypt's air force on the ground. The Israelis took the Sinai Peninsula to the Suez Canal. Twelve thousand Egyptian soldiers died in the attack. This defeat was a blow to Nasser, and he resigned. He returned to his post the following day, following mass demonstrations for his return.

The Egyptian army was in chaos. The country's economy deteriorated. In July 1970, Egypt and Israel finally reached a cease-fire agreement. The stress of these conflicts ruined Nasser's health. By September of the same year, he had died of a massive heart attack. His funeral drew about 4 million mourners, more than any other funeral had in history. His government had many failings, but it gave Egypt a sense of national pride and raised the standard of living for millions of Egyptians.

Anwar Sadat

Nasser's vice president, Anwar Sadat, succeeded him. In 1973,

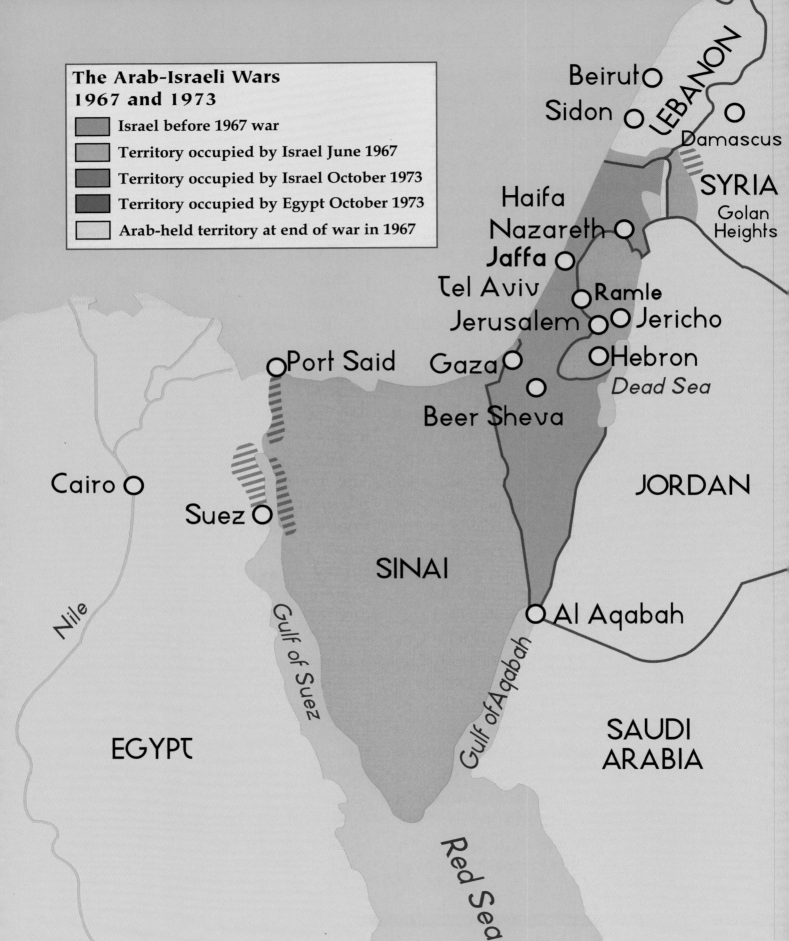

The Arab-Israeli Wars 1967 and 1973

- Israel before 1967 war
- Territory occupied by Israel June 1967
- Territory occupied by Israel October 1973
- Territory occupied by Egypt October 1973
- Arab-held territory at end of war in 1967

Beirut

Sidon

LEBANON

Damascus

SYRIA

Golan Heights

Haifa

Nazareth

Jaffa

Tel Aviv

Ramle

Jerusalem

Jericho

Gaza

Hebron

Dead Sea

Port Said

Beer Sheva

JORDAN

Cairo

Suez

SINAI

Al Aqabah

Nile

Gulf of Suez

Gulf of Aqabah

SAUDI ARABIA

EGYPT

Red Sea

another war with Israel weakened the economy. Food shortages led to riots. Sadat went to Jerusalem to talk to the Israelis. A real solution for peace in the region would help him gain foreign investments. In September 1978, Egypt signed peace accords with Israel. The other Arab nations had expected Sadat to speak for all of them. Instead, he made a separate peace between Israel and Egypt. Egypt lost its place in the Arab League and the Arab world. Sadat lost the sympathy of Egypt's most extreme Islamic groups.

On coming to power, Sadat had freed the Muslim Brotherhood. Founded during the economic depression, the Society of Muslim Brotherhood was an Islamic fundamentalist group. Their leader was a schoolteacher named Sheikh Hasan al-Banna. Al-Banna taught his followers to work for the common good and obey the word of God. The Muslim Brotherhood helped people help themselves through

advancements in education and increased job opportunities. The group soon became a major political force. In October 1954, someone had tried to assassinate Nasser. He blamed the Muslim Brotherhood and outlawed the group.

Tensions between the Arab world and Israel had increased since Israel was recognized as an independent nation in 1948. From then on, fighting between Arabs and Israelis had frequently erupted in the Middle East, especially in and around Egypt. The map (left) shows areas occupied by Arabs and Israelis from 1967 to 1973. Israeli territorial gains made during the 1967 Six-Day War between Israel and Egypt, Jordan, and Syria, are shown in the Gaza Strip, the Sinai Peninsula, the West Bank, and the Golan Heights. Egypt suffered severe human, territorial, and economic losses due to the forced closure of the Suez Canal. Attempts by Arabs to regain these territories resulted in the 1973 Yom Kippur War between a coalition of Egyptian and Syrian forces against Israel. President Anwar Sadat (above) in a photograph taken shortly before his assassination on October 6, 1981, by soldiers in Cairo.

Sadat discouraged the Brotherhood as well as other fundamentalist Islamic groups, yet many Egyptians became more openly religious. Women wore long dresses with long sleeves and head veils. Men wore loose, modest attire. These people opposed Westernizing ideas in appearance and behavior. Although they wanted to be more modern, they did not want to become less Egyptian. Their leaders believed a return to traditional religious values would solve the country's problems.

There were many new Islamic groups like the Brotherhood that taught religion as a basis for Egyptian life. Some tried to work through the government. Others wanted to destroy the government and create a new system. Some used violence. In 1981, a militant Muslim group, the Islamic Jihad of Egypt, assassinated Sadat.

Amid the chaotic aftermath in the streets of Cairo, military officers (left) are seen tending to a man who was wounded in the assassination of President Anwar Sadat. Confusion in the courtroom (right) is evident during the trial of twenty-four Muslim fundamentalists who were charged with the assassination of President Sadat. The trial took place on November 30, 1981, where defendants in the case pleaded innocent to all charges. In this photograph, the defendants are seen shouting to their lawyers and family members from steel restraining cells.

Egyptians, such as this artist and scribe in Cairo, earn a modest living by catering to Egypt's large tourist population. According to statistics provided by the U.S. Central Intelligence Agency (CIA), nearly half of all Egyptian workers have jobs in the service industry, though tourism in the country has fallen sharply since September 2001.

Hosni Mubarak

Hosni Mubarak succeeded Sadat. A highly capable air force officer, Mubarak rebuilt the air force for Nasser after it was destroyed in 1967. In 1975, he became vice president. He is popular among the Egyptians. They reelected him in 1987, 1993, and 1999.

As president, Mubarak wants to improve social and economic equality among the Egyptian people. His government works to create new jobs, attract foreign investments, and develop improved industry.

In 2002, Mubarak inaugurated a new suspended bridge at Aswan. Like Nasser's High Dam, Mubarak sees the bridge as a way for technology to tame the ancient geography of Egypt so that it better serves the Egyptian people. In Upper Egypt, new projects are underway from Beni Suef to Abu Simbel. These will assist with the tourism that supports much of southern Egypt.

One of Mubarak's greatest recent concerns is the United States's war against Iraq. In 2003, the United States took military action against Iraq because the country was accused of not complying with rules regarding weapons of mass destruction. Mubarak agreed that Iraq should not harbor these weapons but believed armed conflict would plunge the entire Middle East into economic depression. In an October 2002 press conference, he insisted that striking Iraq would not intimidate or bring peace to the Arab world and would only lead to more problems.

The Islamic Jihad

The Islamic Jihad of Egypt has two factions. In early 2003, the leader of one, Ayman al-Zawahiri, was in Afghanistan as part of Osama bin Ladin's allegedly weakened World Islamic Front. The other, the Vanguards of Conquest (New Jihad Group), follows the leadership of Ahmad Husayn Agiza. Both want to overthrow the present-day

An Egyptian student at Cairo University with his face covered in a white sheet mask and a bandanna that reads "Qassam Brigades" (the military wing of the Palestinian Islamic militant group Hamas) holds a mock missile as he stands in front of banners calling for jihad, or "holy war." A poster showing President George W. Bush is seen in the background during a rally to condemn the United States–led invasion of Iraq in March 2003. More than 1,500 students attended the rally held at the Cairo University campus, which was ringed by thousands of riot police.

(*From left to right*) King Abdullah II of Jordan, his wife, Queen Rania, Egyptian first lady Suzanne Mubarak, and Egyptian president Hosni Mubarak in Cairo on April 14, 2003. Abdullah and his wife arrived in Egypt for a brief visit to discuss developments in the Middle East following the fall of the regime of Iraqi president Saddam Hussein.

Egyptian government of President Hosni Mubarak and replace it with an Islamic state. Their larger goal is to end Western influence in Muslim countries.

The Islamic Jihad specializes in armed attacks on high-level Egyptian officials. In addition to Sadat, they claim responsibility for the attempted assassinations of Interior Minister Hassan Al-Alfi in August 1993 and Prime Minister Atef Sedky in November 1993.

They have also targeted Israelis, Westerners, and various Christian leaders on Egyptian soil. Many Coptic Christians have immigrated to the United States to escape their attacks.

Egypt's security forces take the Islamic Jihad very seriously. Under former Minister of Interior General Zaki Badr, 8,000 Jihad activists were imprisoned. In October 1990, General Abd Al-Hadim Moussa declared, "The security forces have committed themselves to the complete elimination of the Jihad organization in Egypt."

In June 1992, the Jihad murdered Faraj Fodah, an author who supported Israeli-Egyptian peace. Since 1993, the group has not conducted an attack inside Egypt. However, it has threatened the United States for imprisoning Sheikh Umar Abd al-Rahman, whom it regards as its spiritual leader. Rahman, together with Abbud al-Zumar (the leader of the original Jihad, who is currently imprisoned in Egypt) has recently called for a "peaceful front."

The Future

Egypt's economy improved impressively in the 1990s. The country tamed inflation and attracted more investments from foreign nations. Egyptian oil was part of this economic success. There are forty oil-producing fields in the Gulf of Suez. The October field contains 1.5 billion barrels of recoverable oil. Several others contain as much as 700 million barrels each.

At the beginning of the twenty-first century, Egypt's economic improvement slowed. Although Mubarak's administration promises long-term gains, his many projects are

expensive. In addition, tourism has suffered since the terrorist attacks on the United States on September 11, 2001. This has affected the economies of many countries in the region.

The Middle East is an area of great political complexity. When the Egyptians freed themselves from the British in 1952, they gained an overwhelming sense of Arab nationalism. History was with them, but Iraq was not. In 1978, Sadat's peace with Israel alienated many Arabs and cost Egypt its place in the Arab League. Egypt has worked to repair this damage. In the coming years, it could provide peaceful leadership in a region intensified by conflicts.

Egypt's greatest source of wealth and strength has always been its land. The rich Nile Valley made Egypt a great civilization. Its natural boundaries offered safety and national identity. During almost 2,000 years of foreign rule—long before the modern idea of nationalism—Egyptians saw themselves as the people of Egypt.

This land is both precious and necessary to Egypt's ongoing health as an economy and as a nation. The current government needs to ensure its many projects do not do more damage to the environment. Much

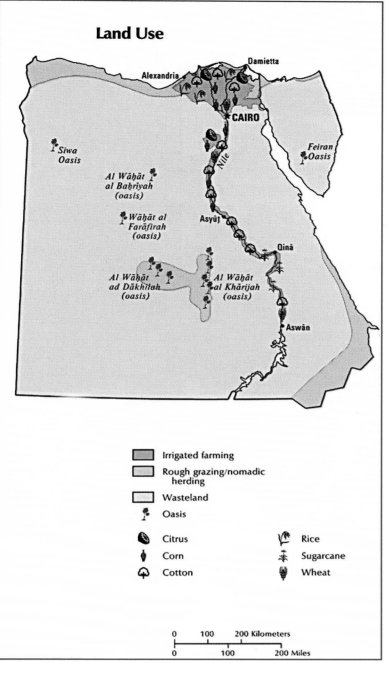

Land Use

Damietta

Alexandria

CAIRO

Nile

Siwa Oasis

Al Wāḥāt al Baḥriyah (oasis)

Wāḥāt al Farāfirah (oasis)

Asyūţ

Feiran Oasis

Al Wāḥāt ad Dākhilah (oasis)

Al Wāḥāt al Khārijah (oasis)

Qinā

Aswân

■	Irrigated farming
▨	Rough grazing/nomadic herding
□	Wasteland
☘	Oasis

Citrus		Rice	
Corn		Sugarcane	
Cotton		Wheat	

```
0        100      200 Kilometers
|----|----|----|----|
0        100      200 Miles
```

As it was during ancient times, nearly all of Egypt's current farmland remains in its fertile Nile Valley and delta. In contrast, 98 percent of Egypt's land is actually part of a vast plateau that is subject to droughts, windstorms, earthquakes, and seasonal flooding. Egypt's recent surge in population has also put added stress on its limited natural resources.

farmland has been lost to urbanization. Nasser's High Dam prevents rich Nile silt from reaching the fields. Oil pollution threatens coral reefs and beaches. Pesticides and sewage pollute the water and rapid population growth strains the country's resources.

The challenge for Egypt as it moves forward will be to maximize its place in the international and Arab worlds while protecting its lands, its resources, and its people.

TIMELINE

3200 BC Egyptians develop first hieroglyphs.

3150 BC Egypt becomes a unified kingdom.

3000 BC Upper and Lower Egypt are united, beginning the Early Dynastic Period.

2630 BC Egyptians build Step Pyramid for King Djoser.

2613 BC Mesopotamian city-states unite under one king.

525 BC Persians conquer kingdom of Egypt.

332 BC Alexander the Great conquers Egypt

31 BC Cleopatra and Mark Antony are defeated by Octavian. Egypt falls under Roman rule.

AD 639 Arab domination in Egypt; introduction of Arabic language in Egypt.

1096 The beginning of the Crusades against Islam.

1250 Mamluks seize power in Egypt.

1347 Plague first appears in Egypt.

1798 Napoléon Bonaparte arrives in Egypt.

1801 British and Turkish Ottomans invade Egypt.

1869 Completion of the Suez Canal.

1882 British move into Egypt.

1914 Britain declares Egypt a protectorate state; World War I begins.

1918 World War I ends.

1921 Egyptian nationalists push for an independent Egypt.

1922 Britain declares Egypt's independence; Ahmed Fuad becomes king.

1923 Egyptian constitution is approved.

1936 King Fuad is succeeded by his son, Faruk.

1939 Start of World War II; Egypt is instrumental in Britain's defense strategy.

1946 Egyptians oppose the push to create a national Jewish state.

1947 Nation of Israel is formed.

1948 Egyptians send troops to defend Palestinians in Israel.

1950 Gamal Abdel Nasser forms a group to overthrow the Egyptian government.

1952 Nasser's "Free Officers" stage a coup and seize power; King Faruk is exiled.

1953 Egypt is declared a republic under President Muhammad Naguib.

1954 Nasser ousts Naguib.

1956 The Suez Canal is nationalized.

1957 Reforms in Egypt improve education and job opportunities.

1966 Arab Socialist Party becomes the sole political party in Egypt.

1967 Israel attacks Egypt, Jordan, and Syria and reaches the Suez Canal.

1968 Israeli forces nearly eliminate the Egyptian military; 11,500 Egyptian casualties.

1970 Nasser dies; Anwar Sadat is elected Egyptian president.

1973 Egypt launches a surprise attack against Israeli forces in the Suez Canal.

1974 Israeli-Egyptian agreement calls for Israeli withdrawal from the Sinai Peninsula.

1978 Sadat and Menachem Begin sign the Camp David Accords.

1981 Sadat is assassinated by Islamic extremists.

1982 Hosni Mubarak is elected president of Egypt.

1991 Persian Gulf War begins; Egypt is part of the thirty-four-nation alliance against Iraq.

1996 Islamic militants attack in Luxor, Egypt; tourism in Egypt slows.

2000 Egypt's National Democratic Party (NDP) dominates the nation's politics.

2001 Mubarak enters his third decade in power; NDP remains strong. Bibliotheca Alexandria opens.

2002 Mubarak urges a complete withdrawal of Israelis from Arab lands that were occupied in 1967 as a further step toward peace in the region.

2003 Anti-war protests in Cairo draw thousands of supporters urging the withdrawal of U.S. troops from Iraq.

GLOSSARY

Byzantine Empire The Eastern Roman or Greek Empire that ruled Egypt until the Arab invasion of AD 639.

caliph A successor of Muhammad who is the secular and spiritual head of Islam.

cataract A waterfall or descent of a river over rocks; the six rocky areas of the middle Nile Valley between Aswan and Khartoum.

convert To change from one religious belief to another.

Copt A Christian Egyptian of pre-Islamic Egypt or member of the Coptic Church.

coup (coup d'état) A french term meaning "blow to the state" that refers to a sudden, unexpected overthrow of a government by outsiders.

Crusades Military expeditions undertaken by European Christians in the eleventh, twelfth, and thirteenth centuries to recover the Holy Land of Palestine from the Muslims.

decolonization A nation's shift from colonial to independent status.

delta The area encompassed by the fan-shaped branching of the Nile tributaries in Lower Egypt.

dynasty Succession of rulers from the same family or line.

Hellenism A devotion to or imitation of ancient Greek thought, customs, or styles, including classical ideas.

Islam A monotheistic religion that worships Allah and follows the teachings of the prophet Muhammad.

Lower Egypt The region centered on the Delta; its symbol was papyrus.

Mamluk A member of a military slave caste of Turkish origin.

martyr Person, usually religious, who dies for what he or she believes.

Memphis Capital city of ancient Egypt.

mercenary Soldier who fights for pay.

Middle Kingdom Egyptian history covering the years 2040 to 1750 BC.

New Kingdom The period of Egyptian history from 1550 to 1086 BC.

nomads People without a fixed home, like the wandering tribes of the Arabian Desert; Bedouins.

Old Kingdom The period of Egyptian history from 2686 to 2160 BC.

Ottoman Empire Turkish empire that ruled Egypt as a province from 1517 to 1914.

papyrus A tall water plant that was used to make paper.

Rosetta stone Three-foot-high stone monument dating back to 196 BC, in which three different scripts—hieroglyphic, demotic, and Greek—represent the same text; a message of thanks to Pharaoh Ptolemy V.

sultan An Arab ruler; the word means "power" in Arabic.

ulama A religious leader.

Upper Egypt The southern part of the country extending along the Nile from Memphis to the cataracts; its symbol was the lotus, or water lily.

Valley of the Kings A valley on the west bank of the Nile River near Luxor, which contains the tombs of many pharaohs.

vizier A high-level political advisor; usually the most powerful person in power after the king.

wali Egyptian viceroy under the Ottomans.

FOR MORE INFORMATION

The Embassy of the Arab Republic
    of Egypt
3521 International Court NW
Washington, DC 20008
(202) 895-5400
Web site: http://www.
    embassyofegyptwashingtondc.org

The Oriental Institute of the University
    of Chicago
1155 East 58th Street
Chicago, IL 60637
(773) 702-9514
Web site: http://www-oi.uchicago.edu/
    OI/default.html

Web Sites

Due to the changing nature of Internet
links, the Rosen Publishing Group, Inc.,
has developed an online list of Web sites
related to the subject of this book. This
site is updated regularly. Please use this
link to access the list:

http://www.rosenlinks.com/liha/egyp

FOR FURTHER READING

Aykroyd, Clarissa. *Egypt: Modern Middle East Nations and Their Strategic Place in the World*. Brookshire, Texas: Mason Crest Publishers, 2003.

Barghusen, Joan D., and Bob Moulder. *Daily Life in Ancient and Modern Cairo*. Minneapolis: Runestone Press, 2001.

Hobbs, Joseph J. *Egypt: Modern World Nations*. New York: Chelsea House Publishing, 2002.

Stanley, Diane. *Saladin: Noble Prince of Islam*. New York: HarperCollins Children's, 2002.

BIBLIOGRAPHY

Al-Sayyid Marsot, Afaf Lutfi. *A Short History of Modern Egypt*. Cambridge, England: Cambridge University Press, 1998.

Bowman, Alan K. *Egypt After the Pharaohs: 332 BC–AD 642, from Alexander to the Arab Conquest*. Los Angeles: University of California Press, 1986.

Brander, Bruce. *The River Nile*. Washington, DC: National Geographic Society, 1966.

Breasted, Henry James. *A History of Egypt: From the Earliest Times to the Persian Conquest*. New York: Bantam Books, 1964.

Dee, Jonathan. *Chronicles of Ancient Egypt*. London: Collins & Brown, 1998.

Griggs, C. Wilfred. *Early Egyptian Christianity: From Its Origins to 451 CE*. Boston: Brill, 2000.

Hitti, Philip K. *History of the Arabs: From the Earliest Times to the Present*, tenth edition. New York: St. Martin's Press, 1970.

Ruffle, John. *The Egyptians: An Introduction to Egyptian Archaeology*. Ithaca, NY: Cornell University Press, 1977.

Stewart, Desmond. *The Pyramids and Sphinx*. New York: Newsweek Book Division, 1971.

Vrettos, Theodore. *Alexandria: City of the Western Mind*. New York: The Free Press, 2001.

INDEX

About the Author

Allison Stark Draper is a freelance writer living in upstate New York.

Acknowledgment

Special thanks to Karin van der Tak for her expert guidance regarding matters pertaining to the Middle East.

Photo Credits

Cover (map), pp. 1 (foreground), 1 (background), 4–5 © Geoatlas; cover (background), pp. 18, 44–45, 50 © Bettmann/Corbis; cover (top left), p. 54 (right) © AP/Wide World Photos; cover (bottom left) © The Art Archive/Tate Gallery London/Eileen Tweedy; cover (bottom right), pp. 14, 15 (inset), 16, 22 © AKG London/Erich Lessing; pp. 6, 32–33, 52 maps designed by Tahara Hasan; pp. 8, 19, 27, 41 © Mary Evans Picture Library; p. 10 © Gianni Dagli Orti/Corbis; pp. 13, 31, 36 (inset), 38, 42–43, 46 © AKG/London; pp. 14–15, 20, 21, 24, 36, 40, 48–49, 59 courtesy of the General Libraries, the University of Texas at Austin; p. 25 © Adam Woolfitt/Corbis; pp. 28–29 © Archivo Iconografico, S.A./Corbis; p. 37 © AKG London/Doris Poklekowski; p. 47 © The Library of Congress, Geography and Map Division; pp. 48–49 courtesy of the United Nations Cartographic Section; pp. 53, 54 (left) © Kevin Fleming/Corbis; p. 55 © Peter Sanders; pp. 56, 57 © AFP/Corbis.

Series Designer: Tahara Hasan; **Editor:** Joann Jovinelly;
Photo Researcher: Elizabeth Loving